TRUE TO THE END

by
Joe Quinlivan

An Emigrant's story

This book is for the many hundreds of thousands of Irish men and women who were forced to emigrate and leave family and friends behind particularly in the 1950s and 60s. Included in this dedication are the parents of those emigrants who had to say a painful goodbye to their sons and daughters.

TRUE TO THE END

A catalogue record for this book is available from the
British Library

ISBN 978-0-9934230-0-0

Published by Joe Quinlivan
For more copies of this book, please email
joe.quinlivan@yahoo.co.uk

Designed, Set and Printed by Modern Printers, Unit 11B,
Loughboy Industrial Estate, Kilkenny, Ireland.
sales@modernprinters.ie

Preface

This book marks a personal story of the experience of an Irishman who lived through one of the most defining periods in recent Irish history, the mass exodus from Ireland and in particular rural Ireland in the 1950's.

There is a shocking graphic in the 1961 Census of Population of the population pyramid for rural Ireland and for the population as a whole. The population pyramid describes the share of the population by age group. As the mortality rate is low until higher ages, the pyramid should be steep at younger ages and then fall in older ages. However, the 1961 population pyramid for rural Ireland saw the share of males aged 20-25 as only 40% of the population of the 10-15 age group. In other words, the population of this age group living in rural Ireland was 60% below what one would expect after a decade of emigration. The equivalent reduction in urban areas was about 30%. This story of emigration from rural areas was one of people leaving both for overseas and to the towns and cities.

Over the decade of the 1950's, on average a net 40000 people left Ireland. This compares with 20000 per annum in the 1980's and less than 24000 per annum since the onset of the current economic crisis. It should be noted that the population in 1951 was less than 3 million, compared with 3.4 million in 1981 and 4.2 million in 2006, so the total number of emigrants as a share was both absolutely higher, but relatively much higher. In fact it was not until 2011, that the population in rural Ireland recovered from the 200,000 people who left rural Ireland in the 1950's. In other words, this population shock was nothing more than a calamity, looking more like the impact of a war than a natural population shift.

The story of Joe Quinlivan puts a name and an experience to these incredible statistics. It was an era of lower skills, where Irish people got the lowest skilled jobs and were at the bottom of the heap is economic immigrants in England during the 1950's. I was an emigrant in the 1990's and early 2000's in London. At one stage, I and all other 3 of my siblings were away. Ours was the generation of the "Young Europeans", the famous poster in Dublin airport, where all bar one of those in the poster had emigrated within a year. While the reasons for emigration were similar, a lack of jobs and high unemployment at home, the context was very different for my generation. Many of the emigrants of my generation had third level qualifications and we settled into professional employment. Gone too, largely was the visible discrimination against the Irish, although it was difficult at times, particularly during the earlier part of my time in London.

Although things were undoubtedly easier for my generation, many of the issues remained the same as Joe's. We missed our families and our native country. We have a lot in common with the British, with a shared history and language, culturally we are different. I very much empathised with Joe's experience of a difference in humour and outlook. One of my first experiences was standing at the bottom of a non-functioning Jubilee Line escalator with my 6 bags, (in the days when emigrants weren't charged excess baggage charges), where I was passed for 10 minutes by Londoners, before an Australian couple offered to help me carry my bags up.

For much of my time in London, travel home was easier than Joe's generation, although we were not quite the Ryanair generation, who can hop over and back with airfares similar to bus fares. I endured that horrible journey by bus and ferry from Limerick to London more times than I like to remember. Nevertheless it wasn't the story of overcrowded bumpy cold ferries of the 1950's.

Communication with home was easier, we had the cheap phone cards, rather than the Skype and email we have now. Our version of the Clare Champion being posted out was the IrishTimes.com on the internet, which was a fantastic resource. Our generation had the Irish pub, dances in Irish Centres and sporting weekends in common with Joe's, although by my generation, the Irish pub and traditional music was very cool in London.

I lived in similar areas, close to Kilburn, where 1000's of Irish had visited before, although we differentiated ourselves as living in South Hampstead/Abbey Road instead of Kilburn High Road, which was only about 400m away. I have an abiding memory of the remnants of the earlier migrant generation of being transitory. Many that I met, retained their accents, interests and surrounded themselves with Irish friends, looking from a distance at a former life in Ireland.

This generation in many cases did not have the same opportunities to return to Ireland that we had. 3 of my family were able to return once the Irish economy picked up again, with only one remaining with his British family in Liverpool. This was a story of thousands of Irish who picked up skills in the 1980's and 1990's overseas and drove on the so-called Celtic Tiger. Ironically many of us are probably trapped now in Ireland with the negative equity and big mortgages we acquired once we did come home. Nevertheless I am certainly glad I have been able to live again in Ireland. For all its faults, Ireland is home.

I think as a nation we failed those who were not as fortunate. Hundreds of thousands remained overseas. Of course many, like my brother remained overseas out of choice, many that I met had no choice. In 1991, there were 493000 Irish born in Britain, more than the population of Dublin City at the time. Many of these as we hear in Joe's book had limited eligibility for state pensions, relying on means tested pensions in Britain that were substantially lower than those available in Ireland, since that generation retired from 2000. Thus while the Celtic tiger was at its peak, many from this generation were forced to live in poverty in one of the most expensive cities on Earth. While there has been some expenditure on social service in Irish Centres in the UK, it was a pittance relative to the need. Ironically Ireland has one of the youngest populations on the back of the numbers of those born in Ireland, currently retired, living overseas, resulting in lower public finance pressures.

This generation however is dying off. By 2011, there were 407000, down from a peak of 683000 in 2011.Despite the upsurge in emigration in recent years, the population of the Irish born in Britain has been declining. As Ireland's economy recovers it is important that we do not ignore this group. Recent studies have found many are in poor health.

In addition to looking after the older generations of migrants, we need to plan for a more sustainable economy at home, where those who emigrate do so out of choice and where we can support those who want to stay in Ireland and in particular those who continue to wish to live in rural Ireland. 200000 have left Ireland since the crisis in 2008 (although many returned).

Pat Spillane and I undertook a nationwide consultation a couple of years ago together with colleagues on the Commission for the Economic Development of Rural Areas (CEDRA). The report we produced can be found on www.ruralireland.ie and highlights a number of recommendations to revitalise rural Ireland and enable rural Ireland to contribute to the national recovery. Economic development of rural Ireland has had a relatively low profile in national planning since the turn of the Millennium, despite most of the population living outside of the cities. The emphasis of our report is not about spending more money, but rather targeting more focus and better coordination of development strategies to improve the effectiveness of existing spending on rural economic development.

The government have appointed a new Minister, helped by an inter-departmental group to implement the strategy. I hope it is successful in its mission and help to enable those who wish to, to remain in rural Ireland, rather than having to face the boat of Joe's and my generation.

Prof. Cathal O'Donoghue is Head of the Teagasc Rural Economy and Development Programme, one of Teagasc's 4 research programme areas. He is also adjunct professor in UCD and NUI Galway and Professor (Extra-ordinary) at the University of Maastricht. He has degrees from UCC, the University of Oxford, UCD, and the University of Warwick, with his PhD from The LSE

He previously worked for the Economic and Social Research Institute, the UK Government Economics and Statistics Services, the University of Cambridge and the National University of Ireland, Galway.

Introduction

My name is Joe Quinlivan formerly a native of County Clare, Ireland. I am just one statistic of the many thousands of emigrants who were forced to leave their native shore back in the 1940s, '50s and '60s. Back in the 1950s living in rented accommodation, as we Irish emigrants did, could be a lonely experience. So I would pass the time at night by making written notes of events that happened at work or in the accommodation. Of course it wouldn't be possible to memorise all the things that I've written about had it been the case that I didn't keep notes. They gathered dust for many years and I had them in a case that I had stored away in the loft. I had forgotten about them until it became necessary to dispose of some of the things that had accumulated. They were brown with age and I thought it would be such a pity to shred or burn them so I decided to try writing a book. I had taken a few computer lessons but the fact that I could only type with one finger - I thought 'this is going to be a daunting task'. The following pages are the result of my endeavours.

Golden Wedding 2012
Back Row L-R: Anthony, Annmarie, Claire, Frances
Front Row L-R: Pauline, Bridgetta, Teresa Mary, Joe
and remembering James (deceased)

Index

x

1.
Ireland's History of Emigration

D own through the centuries a lot has been written about Irish emigration; from the unprecedented levels in the mid 1800s at the time of the Great Famine, (1845 – 1849) with figures reaching one and a half million to the mid twentieth century and again in the twenty first century. The 1940s in Ireland was a particularly tough decade with the Second World War (1939 to 1945) followed by the Arctic winter of 1946 - 47. During the war years clothes, food and most other items were rationed so inevitably many people were hungry, hence the reason that emigration started to accelerate and continued throughout the whole of the 1950s and '60s. Ireland joined the European Economic Union (EEC) in 1973 having failed to join in both 1961 and 1967. Even though the initial efforts were unsuccessful the Government continued to improve the economy in preparation for acceptance. Joining the EEC is seen by many as the catalyst to economic recovery in Ireland. Oil crises in 1973 and 1979 saw a downturn in the world economy which affected Ireland and the country was once again plunged into recession, with interest rates reaching the high teens and emigration once again on the agenda. The Irish economy began to improve during the 1990's culminating in one of the fastest growing economies in the world during the 2000s. This era, which became known as the *'Celtic Tiger'* years, saw Ireland become a country to which former emigrants returned to, and young people from other countries saw as a place of opportunity and one to which they could emigrate. 2008 saw a major upheaval in world banking which filtered through to Ireland and this combined with inflated house prices and other unorthodox practices saw a major collapse in the Irish economy culminating, once again, in the exodus of the young people of Ireland to foreign lands.

Emigration has affected so many Irish families and the current surge continues the pain and grief as the youth exit Ireland on a daily basis. The blight of emigration seems to have lingered over Ireland for many centuries erupting from time to time. It is a bit like a volcano, in that it dies down, eases off for a period of time and then erupts again with varying degrees of ferocity.

It has always been the case that people move from one country to another to set up home, take up better paid employment or for various other reasons. However, the vast majority of those who moved away from Ireland in the late 1940s and '50s did not have any alternative due to the lack of employment opportunities and the austere conditions under which they were living Emigration levels from Ireland during this period were very high both to Great Britain and America but particularly to Great Britain. Unfortunately, many of the men and women who emigrated in the 1950s are no longer with us for various reasons and they have become the forgotten generation, even by the Irish Government.

Perhaps emigration could be split into three different categories - voluntary, obligatory and progressive; but for most emigration was obligatory, while for some it was both obligatory and progressive. For example emigrants whose intended destination was America or Australia would go to the United Kingdom (UK) and work there for some time in order to generate the necessary finance to complete stage two of the originally intended destination. It was particularly difficult for a parent or parents who had only one offspring who would decide to emigrate to America or Australia. Australia was approximately a six week journey by boat so in the event of a family member passing away it would be difficult to return. While the current emigrants from Ireland are leaving due to the lack of work and opportunities, there are many young people who are leaving voluntarily and are treating emigration as a working holiday. They stay and work in a particular country for a while and then move on to the next one.

I decided to write this story from my own experiences and recollections of emigration, and because of the high levels of emigration that took place from the surrounding area where I lived. Twelve young people emigrated from my town-land, Tubber, Co Clare in the early 1950s and that was approximately twenty five per cent of the total number of people (all ages) living in the neighbourhood. This was pretty much the same pattern throughout the parish and indeed throughout rural Ireland but of course numbers varied somewhat. I think it would be fair to say that we

- the emigrants - could perhaps be described as refugee's fleeing our native land. Most of the emigrants at that time (and I am sure the same still holds) would have preferred to stay at home but for some it was necessary for survival. For most young people it was a case of leaving school and hanging about doing odd jobs for neighbours for a few bob from time to time, but the few bob wasn't always theirs to keep. For some, their parents may have been struggling to pay outstanding bills so the odd job money would be handed over. Others helped their parents doing farming chores, but of course no money would change hands. Young people in their late teens and early twenties never had permanent paid employment, so packing up their bits and pieces and moving away to some foreign land became inevitable. Emigration was Ireland's greatest export at that time.

Emigration had a huge effect on many families fragmenting many of them. Every time a family member left home to emigrate it was like a funeral without a coffin. I use the word funeral in that the pain and sadness of losing a family member was almost as great as going to a cemetery to bury him or her. The only difference was that there was a glimmer of hope that some day he or she would return. There is an old saying, '*There is hope from the ocean but none from the grave.*' Leaving home, family and friends was difficult enough but then being confronted with the transition hurdle on arrival at their chosen destination was even more challenging. A completely different way of life was indeed a culture shock for most and it took some time to adjust, particularly for the people from rural Ireland. Employment, transport, accommodation and life in general in the new world for most emigrants were a complete departure from what they left behind. The sound of the then familiar corncrake was gone and the London Underground system had a different lay-out to the *underground* system in rural Ireland which was mainly frequented by moles, rabbits, and badgers!

The 1940s and '50s exit had a devastating effect on many communities in that many neighbourhoods lost most of its young people. Many of my school friends went to America. The popular destinations were New York, Boston, Chicago and a few other big cities in North America but the vast majority went to Great Britain.

Shipping companies operating between Ireland and Britain were kept busy due to the thousands fleeing the country hoping for a better future on the *'other side of the pond'*, meaning the Irish Sea between Ireland and Great Britain. Any employment that gave a bit of independence was welcome despite the fact that people were parted from their family and friends. Most of my school colleagues decided at a very early age that staying in their native land didn't offer any kind of a prosperous future for them although many had the same problem as I had which was lack of education. Nevertheless, they were willing to move on and explore any opportunity that came their way, albeit in a foreign land. Most were bright intelligent young people who had plenty to offer given the opportunity. The cream of Ireland's youth was queuing up to exit the country. It was difficult for many young people endeavouring to adjust to a new culture, a new way of life but courage and determination saw them through and failure for most was never on their agenda.

Some young people were fortunate enough to receive secondary school education in Ireland at that time and the funds for same were, in many instances, provided by older family members who had already emigrated. The down side was that when they had completed their education there was no employment available to reward them for their efforts - so many were forced to cross the sea. The plus side for these people who were forced to emigrate was that it was much easier to secure worthwhile employment which gave them status and financial reward. The youth that are currently emigrating to countries all over the world have advantages over many former emigrants. Most emigrants currently leaving Ireland are educated and articulate and can communicate daily with their families in Ireland through *'Skype or Viber'* if they so wish and many have work experience gained from the boom years of the *'Celtic Tiger'*.

I was always glad to return to my native place to visit my family and during those visits I saw great changes taking place in County Clare. Those changes commenced from about the mid 1970s onwards and of course were not just in my county but throughout Ireland. Ireland was slowly emerging from decades or even centuries of poverty and darkness. New houses, schools and churches started springing up throughout the land. Farming practices began to change and instead of the horse and plough, tractors were now becoming a more popular way of carrying out the farm work. Development was slow and it was almost another 30 years before it peaked and ultimately crashed. For many thousands of emigrants this evolution was many years too late!

Living standards in Ireland remained below their European counterparts until into the 1990s and some emigrants began to return towards the end of this decade. The auld *'Céad Mile Fáilte'* that many returning emigrants expected had long since evaporated. Some emigrants did return home to take over the farms from their elderly parents who in many cases were no longer able to carry on the farming business.

The countryside still has many examples of abandoned and desolate properties which are, in most cases, the legacy of emigration. Many of the old homesteads in rural Ireland fell into a state of disrepair when parents passed away and the family members who left didn't return home. There are still many of these skeletons throughout the country particularly in the west of Ireland which are visited and photographed by the grandchildren and great-grandchildren of the people who once lived in them and who make what could be described as an annual pilgrimage from many countries but particularly from America. Photographs or conversations never fully compensate for actually visiting the old homesteads of their ancestors. I was holidaying in my native County Clare in the mid 1970s and I met a young American brother and sister who were visiting the remains of their grand-parents old home. Their dad emigrated to Boston in the 1940s. They said to me, *'We feel that we have trod on sacred ground where our grand-parents once worked and lived.'* They also said, *'Old photographs or images are no substitute for making the trip and actually seeing at first hand the old homestead and surroundings. We find it difficult to comprehend how people survived without electricity or any electrical appliances.'* They were very emotional and they showed me a small piece of whitewashed stone that they were taking back to America. They also told me about a small window complete with glass and a door that they removed from the building and were having shipped back to America. To them the journey and these treasures were priceless!

Regardless of how long people have been exiled most like to return to their old homestead and the neighbourhood where they were reared. Surroundings may have changed and most friends and neighbours long since departed, but tracing one's childhood steps is always important to any returning emigrant in that it rekindles memories of where and how they spent their early days.

From 1945 to the end of the 1950s it is estimated that some 500,000 Irish men and women left Ireland. Three out of every four emigrants leaving Ireland were headed for Britain. In 1950, some 41,000 people left Ireland. The massive haemorrhaging of young people had a profound effect on the Irish economy in that it remained stagnant for many decades until the era of the 'Celtic Tiger'. Of course it was very good to see Ireland in the fast lane with the rest of Europe and overtaking some of their neighbours along the way although, it was pretty short lived.

Although the introduction of the 'Celtic Tiger' meant wealth and prosperity for the country it also changed the culture and many of the old cherished values were lost. The authentic Irish welcome seemed to have vanished. The friendly neighbour who always made time to have a chat melted away. The open door and the teapot on the hearth, always ready to welcome the visitor also disappeared. Religion became somewhat diluted although many people still attend Church on Sunday, but numbers have diminished considerably over the years. As people grew wealthier they also became rather greedy in many cases. Land and property prices accelerated to the point that many emigrants whose intention it was to return home were priced out of the market.

When the 'Celtic Tiger' roared into town it emerged that there was a shortage of skilled labour so the Irish government endeavoured to get emigrants to return by offering incentives. They also had to recruit skilled labour from many European countries to fill vacancies. For the many emigrants that did return, life was good for a number of years but when the downturn came and the 'Celtic Tiger' stopped roaring some regretted ever coming back. For many who had been away for quite a while returning to Ireland caused similar problems to those which occurred when they originally left home. It was a kind of emigration in reverse. They would have made many new friends abroad and their children would have to leave their school friends behind. That process also split up families in that some of the parents would return and take some of the younger family members with them while other family members remained behind.

Again history is being repeated in that emigration is on the menu yet again with vast numbers leaving Ireland since 2010. Current emigration levels are not expected to reach that of the 1950s but parents are once again confronted with the breakup of families and the grief and sadness is no less than in previous times. Almost certainly people that left Ireland back in the 1950s made a considerable contribution to creating wealth and boosted the economies of the countries that they moved to, and no doubt it will be the same today.

Little Ode to Lissycasey   By Joe Quinlivan

Lissycasey is a village
In the mid- west County Clare
Where life has become more affluent
For the people living there.

Situated on the main road
Between Ennis and Kilkee
Sure this Lissycasey village
Isn't the place it used to be.

Out went the auld paraffin lamp
When along came the electric light
Sure 'twas a God-send for all the farmers
When cows would be calving at night.

Gone are the days of the horse and cart
When they trundled through the village
Some carrying milk in creamery cans
And others dung for tillage.

The bus service through the village
Is the good old CIE
It runs a daily service
Between Limerick and Kilkee.

It has a well-known pub
That the local's just call Fanny's
Famous for its egg flips
From the days of our great-grannies.

Then there is the Boree Log
Where once stood Melican's pub
'tis a place for people to socialise
Or for a drink and a bit of grub.

Spring water was found deep underground
In a place that was once Pappy Mac's field
And there now stands a modern facility
Where the water is bottled and sealed.

The discovery of this spring water
Has put Lissycasey on the map
And the purity and quality of the product
Will replace the piped water to the tap.

The water that's brought to the surface
Is from a distillery deep underground
Sure 'tis a boon for the whole community
That this buried treasure was found.

For it there is no substitute
To quench or ease ones thirst
The coolness and quality of the water
Puts 'Clare Spring' way out first.

Lissycasey's dead centre is a cemetery
A place that's quite unique
In that villagers are dyin' to get in there
Almost every week.

It has a famous address called High Street
On the banks of Glough a Crow
But 'tis a High Street with a difference
Where many visitors do not go.

But to the people of Lissycasey
Continue to forge ahead
And one day your famous village
Will become a town instead.

2.
Early Experiences

I was born in Lissycasey which is a small parish in County Clare in 1936. My father's name was James and my mother Mary (nee Reidy), both now dead RIP, I have a sister Mary and a brother Michael. I left National School in 1950 at thirteen and half years of age with a poor standard of education which was comparable with many thousands of others. Ireland didn't have anything to offer me in terms of employment or a secure future as at that time the country was still in the slow lane by comparison to its European neighbours.

For the next four years it proved impossible for me to get full time or even part time employment. I did however work for farmers in spring and summer for short periods in the bog or saving hay. Sometimes I didn't get paid and sometimes it was, '*God spare you the health.*' On other occasions, '*I'll see you after Mass on Sunday.*' Sometimes I would be paid in instalments. I might get a £1 of the money due or I may never get paid the full amount. Another method would be, '*I'll pay you when I'll sell a couple of cattle*', or '*I'll pay you when I'll get the next creamery cheque.*' In some cases the sale of cattle or receipt of a creamery cheque didn't result in payment for me. It became necessary to carry out a kind of risk assessment as to who might pay before taking on any more bog or meadow work. Of course the problem with too many '*God spare you the health*' payments was that it wasn't possible to cash in any of them! I'm sure most people intended paying, but their good intentions were sometimes overtaken by events.

It became apparent to most teenagers in those days that moving away from Ireland was inevitable, particularly for people from households with up to six or more off-spring. Many people in their late teens or early twenties went from day to day and week to week with small amounts of pocket money in their possession but for many it was empty pockets. For those who had some pocket money it would only amount to a couple of shillings or half a crown, but those with a pound in their pocket would think and feel that they had won the lottery. Looking to the future it was clear that it wouldn't be possible to enter into marriage, have their own home or support a family. Although nobody was starving (not like the people during the great Famine), most didn't have money to buy new clothes or shoes or do the many things that the youth of today take for granted. Not many smoked cigarettes simply because they didn't have the money to buy them, but as a bit of a treat some youths would club together and buy a packet to share between them. Others would make roll ups with dry tea and smoke them.

It was so depressing getting out of bed each day without any sense of purpose. One didn't have any money to go anywhere such as taking a trip to the nearest town or visit a local shop to purchase a little treat. During the winter period most of the time was spent indoors and it could be testing to retain one's sanity in the absence of television or any kind of entertainment. The absence of electricity for much of rural Ireland made it a rather dark and depressing place in which to live. Many endured real hardship especially in some small farming communities, sometimes cold and hungry and without income. Consecutive Irish governments failed to create opportunities or incentives to generate employment or training initiatives to retain the energies of at least some of the youth that emigrated. In my young days of unemployment in Ireland I didn't get unemployment benefit or job seekers allowance. Of course neither did anybody else as it was in the Government's interest not to pay these benefits and allowances for a number of reasons. By not paying unemployment benefit desperate people were forced to emigrate. It kept unemployment figures at a much lower level than would otherwise be the case. People that didn't have any money to spend, through no fault of their own, weren't of any use in the country as far as the Government was concerned. Down through the years the Irish people have always been resilient and eager to push ahead. Always ready for a challenge, they didn't sit at home hoping that someone would come to their rescue but instead emigrated to various parts of the world.

The only alternative for many thousands of young men and women was to pack their few belongings and start on their journey for either Dublin or Cork. Dublin was the place to catch a boat for Holyhead and Cork for that long journey across the Atlantic to New York. The amount of emigration from the country was like a tidal wave or mini tsunami. For many, Great Britain was the more convenient place of refuge as a near neighbour on Ireland's doorstep. The short hop across the Irish Sea by boat was the favourite mode of travel. The travel time and cost being the main factors for heading to Britain. The cost of air travel was prohibitive due to financial constraints and the fact that Aer Lingus had the monopoly on the Dublin –London route.

For many going away for the first time, their belongings may include a Hurley or a musical instrument to enable them to continue practising their old Irish traditions. Packing up the bag didn't take very long in that people didn't have a lot to pack. Many people borrowed a suitcase or even a trunk to pack their belongings. Some of the old suitcases would be a bit battered from use either by friends or other family members and may have a belt, strap or even a bit of twine tied around it. Trunks were mainly used for the longer hauls such as America, Australia or Canada. However, regardless of the destination any bits of clothing or footwear were valuable items to take with one, at least in the short term 'till new funds became available to replace them. The only footwear that some had for the journey out of Ireland were wellington boots and during one boat trip from Dublin to Holyhead I witnessed that. Emigrants were travelling with friends who were returning from holiday and who had secured employment in the construction industry for them, so the wellington boots were worn 'till they had funds to buy new footwear.

Of course I was not alone; thousands had exactly the same experience. Crossing the Irish Sea between Dublin and Holyhead was only two to four hours depending on weather conditions as opposed to approximately a week to cross the Atlantic from Queenstown (now Cobh) to the East Coast of America.

The Queen Mary, the Mauritania and the Franconia were three of the large liners that departed from Queenstown for that long journey across the Atlantic. It was an era of large families such as some in my home parish. There were twenty one members in one unit another had seventeen, one of sixteen and one of fifteen. Of course these numbers were exceptional. However, many households had up to six teenagers and in some cases even more without employment or some source of income such as unemployment benefit or even the odd casual job. Many of these family members emigrated, some to America, some to Britain or even Australia. The parents remained in Ireland and families became fragmented.

In a rather strange way emigration for many opened up a new world particularly in areas that had large Irish communities be it Britain, America or elsewhere. It brought people from many different counties together and that resulted in friendship and marriage, something that wouldn't have happened had they stayed at home. It also resulted in many emigrants marrying other nationalities. One of the scourges of living in remote parts of Ireland, and in particular the western seaboard was the lack of opportunities to make a living which resulted in difficulties in meeting a life partner as so many had left the country.

Although for many the weekly financial reward following emigration was rather low, most were grateful for it taking into consideration the standard of life they left behind in their native land. Many young people had never experienced a bit of independence and been in a position to afford the basic necessities of daily life. Many saw emigration as a stepping-stone away from poverty with the prospects of independence and building a new future.

3.
Finding Work to Finance Emigration

S taying at home was only an existence for most and the inevitable could only be put off for so long. Finding enough money to pay fares and expenses to emigrate, even to Britain was often a struggle for many. As I moved around the UK throughout the 1950s I heard some compelling stories about how difficult it was to scrape up enough cash to pay for a one way ticket out of Ireland.

There were, however, inventive methods used by emigrants to finance their journey out of Ireland in search of employment. A Kerry man, Big Dinny , from near Cahirciveen, with whom I shared accommodation and worked with in Nottingham, England in 1956 - 57 once told me of the problem he had financing his journey out of Ireland. He thought of a rather ingenious way of getting a few pounds to top up what he had managed to scrape together. He was a very modest, authentic type in character and a fine stature of a man. He was only seventeen years old when he left Ireland in the late 1940s, a year or so after the arctic winter. He was the eldest member of a family of 5 sisters and 2 brothers and his dad had passed away so his mam was struggling to make ends meet.

At the weekends he used to borrow a gun from a neighbour and shoot as many rabbits as possible. He'd keep a couple to help feed the family and the rest he'd sell on the Monday of the following week to a butcher in his nearest town Cahirciveen. He saved up the money over a long period but didn't have enough for his fare and expenses to get him to England. A friend of his from a neighbouring town-land was home on holiday from London. The friend told him that he could get him a job in the buildings. He thought it would be a good opportunity to go back with him but he was a bit short of cash and didn't have enough of time to go on another rabbit shooting expedition. He didn't want to borrow money from his friend so he sold an old bicycle that he got from his uncle to a neighbour for £2.00, but he was still a bit short of cash.

The day before his friend was due to return to London he

walked some four miles to Cahirciveen and went along to the butchers where he usually sold rabbits. He walked past the shop a couple of times and waited 'till the shop was busy. Hanging outside the shop were some rabbits and a couple of pig's heads. He had a big oil cloth bag so he took two rabbits and one of the pig's heads and sold them to another butcher at the other end of the town where he sometimes sold rabbits. He said that he felt pretty bad about it but he was desperate to get out of Ireland and find employment to help his mam and siblings. He managed to get to London although his friend had to help out before they completed their journey. His friend got him a job as promised and for the first year he sent almost all his earnings home.

A couple of years later he went home on holiday and went back to see the butcher to explain what he had done and the reason for his light hand. He offered to pay, but the butcher declined the offer in view of the circumstances and thanked him for his honesty. I thought it was a pretty enterprising story!

Recently, I had a letter published in 'Ireland's Own' magazine concerning emigration from Ireland during the 1950s. As a result I received amazing accounts of how people managed to scrape up enough money to get out of Ireland and the type of employment they initially got on arrival. Some worked in the railways, others for farmers and one worked for the Coal Board down the pits. All were happy to have found employment regardless of the austere circumstances that they found themselves in.

I received a very fascinating story via email from an eighty-four year old man now living in California but originally from Wexford on how he financed his journey out of Ireland in 1950. I've kept his email on my computer. He was born in 1929 and told how he worked on a farm but didn't get paid half the time. He said, *'These were the days when you had to go to bed early to get your shirt washed.'* He had his first job when he was eight years old and worked every evening after school and all day Saturday for sixpence. Nothing would catch him when he got paid on a Saturday evening as he would be so desperate to get home to give the sixpence to his mother. His mother required the extra money as she had six children to feed. After buying a loaf of bread there wouldn't be a lot of the sixpence left or it would only pay for part of a second loaf.

When he decided to emigrate he hadn't a penny in his pocket. He walked down a road with his bike and a small *'puck'*, not a word that I'd heard before, of his personal belongings then cycled some forty miles to Dublin to catch the boat to Holyhead in Wales. When he got to the boat he walked up and down endeavouring to sell his bicycle to get money to pay the boat fare. It was eventually sold for £4 and a ticket was bought for Holyhead. He had enough money to get him to Birmingham and when he got there, pawned an old pocket watch and then walked about three miles from Birmingham City Centre to Small Heath. He got digs and a meal, the best he ever got he said. He then registered for food stamps, work and an insurance card. He walked around the area looking at the vacancies for work that was available in factories and finally got a job in a factory sweeping up. He closely observed how some of the machines were operated and soon got a job operating one. From there on he never looked back.

He worked in the UK for some time before going home. When he returned on his first visit he put a new roof on his mother's house with the help of a cousin. He never forgot his young days in Ireland and how his mother struggled to rear the family. He is doing pretty well in Monterey, California and he is still working at eighty-four years of age. In the forty years that he has lived in California he has made twenty seven trips to Ireland. I thought it was a truly remarkable story of willpower and determination to seek a new life.

In 1960 I was in digs in Falkirk with a Mrs Agnes McGee and a cousin of hers who was living in Glasgow came to visit her. His name was Gerry Boyle or Coyle and he told me how he and his friend Owen left Donegal back in the late 1940s. Some of their friends were working on a big Hydro Electric project in the north of Scotland. I believe it was a place called Lock Sloy. They sent a letter to Gerry saying that they could get him and Owen a job where they were working if they could manage to get across to Scotland. Gerry said, *'Sure Jaysus neither I nor Owen had any money to take us anywhere. We used to go out on the odd fishing trip but sure the couple of quid that we got wouldn't keep us in fags and anyway it was too dangerous after some of our friends lost their lives off the coast of Donegal. We had to try something but it was tough leaving home in the circumstances that we left.'*

Owen told his uncle who had a fishing vessel in Killybegs of their dilemma. The uncle said that he would take them to Campbeltown on the West Coast of Scotland. They set out with just the clothes they were wearing but as Gerry said, *'We both brought a big lock of sandwiches and a couple of bottles of milk with us as we knew that we wouldn't be able to buy any grub.'* They set off from Killybegs but after a couple of hours into the journey they were forced to turn back due to gale force winds. Their boat became waterlogged but they managed to get back safely. They stayed in Killybegs Harbour until the following day and then set off again. The crossing was still pretty rough, but they made it to Scotland.

They got to Campbeltown under the cover of darkness and started walking in the direction of Inveraray, as Owen had a friend who was working there. They were walking for a couple of hours along a dark main road that didn't have very much traffic and it started to rain. They got soaked but eventually managed to thumb a lift. The Good Samaritan took them to his place and made them a meal and dried their clothes. They stayed for a few hours and then set off walking and thumbing again. Finally they arrived at Inveraray where they met Owen's friend. He was a foreman in a big construction site and he took them there. He was staying in caravan on site. He went to the local shops and bought some grub and they stayed overnight in what Gerry described as *'a rather cramped wee bit of space'*. Owen's friend gave them some money on the understanding that they would pay it back when they were in a position to do so.

They continued their journey by bus and train to the big Hydro Electric site in the North of Scotland. It took them four days to complete the journey but they were grateful to their friends for finding them employment. Their friends gave them some old clothing and boots to enable them to start work. After some months they paid everybody back the money they got and thanked the people who helped them along the way. Gerry said that it took three months before they had saved any money to send home once they had paid their debts. He said that living conditions were rough and that life was lonely in a rather isolated place but they stayed there for about eighteen months. He said he'll never forget the struggle that he had as a young boy growing up in Ireland in the 1940s. It demonstrates just how desperate some people were to get away from Ireland and find employment.

I heard some other distressing stories from people who were forced to leave Ireland in the 1950s. Some walked for miles carrying their old case and thumbing lifts to get to the boat. Some wouldn't manage to get to the boat in one day so they'd sleep in a hay barn or an outhouse along the way and get a bit of breakfast from the owner of the property in the morning. It was rather distressing for these people having to leave home in such circumstances. Likewise it was distressing for the families at home not being able to communicate with their loved ones or get updates on their progress. It could be up to a couple of weeks or more in some cases before parents would hear from their son and his final destination. I said son as it was unlikely that a daughter would set off walking.

Others had to borrow money from friends to pay their fare in search of a new world. Some were fortunate enough to have family members already in Britain or America to pay their fare out of Ireland. Many were anxious for other family members to make the same journey as they had done before. When I was seventeen years old I recall being in my hometown, Ennis, on a number of occasions exploring the possibility of finding employment but nothing was available. Job Centres didn't exist but of course they were not necessary! At that time when a vacancy became available it was 'who you knew rather than what you knew'. Vacancies were few and far between. I did however see a notice saying 'Wanted Apply Within'. I had seen it on previous visits but on this occasion I thought I should check it out. Perhaps I should have realised that had it been worthwhile employment it would not have been necessary to advertise it for such a long period, particularly in view of the high unemployment in the town at that time.

When I went inside I was taken through to the back yard of the premises. There were boxes of chickens, hens, ducks and geese everywhere waiting to be plucked, while feathers were blowing about the place. A man wearing what appeared to have been a white coat at some point but now badly stained with blood, and feathers and down; (the soft woolly part under feathers) in his hair, ears and beard which looked like white frost, explained what they were looking for. The job on offer was plucking hens and geese and it was payment by results. I could work five days a week for up to ten hours a day. I think from memory that the remuneration packet broke down as follows- four pence per hen for the first ten hens and six pence per hen thereafter. It was six pence per goose for the first ten geese and nine pence per goose thereafter. There was an additional incentive of one shilling and six pence per full bag of feathers on the day. The size of bag and the quantity of feathers required to fill it didn't seem an incentive worth getting excited about.

He explained that it was dry plucking in all cases as wet feathers weren't saleable and they didn't have drying facilities. He said, *'Ah sure once you'd get a little bit of practice you could make yourself a good few pounds as it's possible to pluck four or five hens an hour.'* I wouldn't have considered it a feather in my cap, so to speak, to be employed plucking hens either short or long term! It appeared that they had a big business for oven ready poultry. Those are the rates that were quoted to me so needless to say it wasn't for me. I got the impression that it was a *'fowl'* place to work! The job offer of plucking hens was as near as I got to finding employment in Ireland back in the early 1950s.

There was the occasional job from time to time but it was necessary to be in the right place at the right time. A job vacancy or job opportunity becoming available in the town would be quickly snapped up. People living some distance away from the town were disadvantaged in that they'd rarely be aware of an advertised vacancy. The only alternative was to emigrate, but timing and having the necessary funds to make the move were of the essence.

4.
Breakfast Before a Day in the Bog

As a young lad I worked with farmers in the bog endeavouring to earn a couple of quid for a bit of pocket money and also to help my parents a little. It was hard earned money working long hours and I was on occasions cold wet and hungry. I worked with different farmers but one farmer and his wife in particular were somewhat different from the rest and I worked with them for longer durations than others.

Perhaps I should say at the outset that the couple I'm referring to below were lovely people, generous and kind but pretty typical of many farming couples of that era. They had funny expressions and altogether they were rather unique. It was spring 1950 and I was only thirteen and half years of age when I first went to work in the bog for this couple. I got a £1 per day working from early morning 'till late at night. I worked with them in 1951, 1952 and 1953 for about two to three weeks each year. A £1 per day was the going rate at that time, but for me it was a lot of money. I got many a laugh working with them and I'm sure that anybody who will read this account will also get a good laugh. I kept a little diary at that time and documented funny things that happened from day to day. I was always interested in unique people such as Jack and Nora. I was also interested in how other people sometimes spoke to one another, the funny stories, expressions and things that happened. All during my working life I had a desire to document unusual stories or sayings and of course it has served a purpose.

The gentleman was called Jack and his wife was Nora, not their real names as I don't wish to reveal their true identity. They didn't have a family and both were in their late 50s. I believe they passed away about the early to mid 1970s. The old thatched house has long since gone. When I go home on holiday I sometimes pass by where it used to be. What I'm about to describe was pretty much Jack and Nora's daily routine while I worked there.

In the morning I'd cycle to their house that was quite some distance away. It was a big long house that had a thatched roof, small windows and was pretty dark inside but a welcoming place.

It had three small whitewashed chimneys with smoke usually coming from the centre one as that was the living quarters and kitchen. The whitewashed chimneys looked rather picturesque from a distance in the early morning sunshine. Everything in the kitchen area had a brownish colour. A picture of Saint Anthony which was hanging above the mantelpiece made him very *'browned off'* looking after years of smoke from the turf fire. A picture of the Sacred Heart hanging on another wall had much the same problem as Saint Anthony. The problem was that they used to get a bit of blow down from time to time when the smoke came back down the chimney and went out over the half door. Some mornings the old paraffin lamp would still be burning at nine o'clock in the dark kitchen, 'till the full door was opened. However, the light from the old lamp wouldn't dazzle anybody in that the globe was usually black. Some mornings when I'd arrive at the house Nora would say, *'Oh are you here already. Himself is down in the cow-house milking.'*

She was a big woman with a bit of a moustache - a heavy growth of hair in her upper lip. At first I was rather afraid of her as her looks were rather intimidating but when I got to know her she was truly a good hearted woman. She would be in a bit of a flap as calves and pigs would be roaring for breakfast. At that time of the morning she'd be in full uniform-wellington boots, a crossover pinafore and a head scarf. The pinafore was fairly well decorated but not with medals. It had a selection of safety pins, needles with bits of thread of various colours and other bits and pieces which decorated it. Her teeth weren't very plentiful as she only had one or two here and there. The ones that she had were yellowish in colour and would have benefited from a bit of a sand blasting. However she always carried a few spares in her pocket but rarely used them.

She sometimes smoked a clay pipe when she'd have money for tobacco or when she got some from Jack. Morning was always a busy time for all the farming community and Jack's place was no different. It was the farmyard rush hour with animals and poultry milling about. Jack would be tripping back and forward to the cow-house with buckets of milk as that was one of his morning chores to milk the cows. I said he'd be tripping and that was the case as

20

he rarely laced his shoes 'till after breakfast. The creamery tank would be gradually filled as Jack milked the cows. He'd have a white perforated cloth tied around the top of the tank to strain the milk. Nora would usually remain indoors preparing fodder for the calves, pigs and poultry and get some breakfast ready. Jack would say to me most mornings '*Good morning young man Jaysus you're early today. You'll need to wait a while now and herself will make you an auld sup of tae and something to ate. You know you can't go to work on an empty stomach. Sure Jaysus we'll all have an auld bite of breakfast when I'm finished milking, I'm ready for a bit of packing myself.*' He'd look up at the sky saying, '*Will it be a day for the bog? Tell herself to make you an auld drop of tae just now 'till I finish milking.*' When I'd tell Nora what Jack said she'd reply, '*Sure the Lord save us that man knows that I have a pot of gruel hanging over the fire for the calves I can't boil the kettle right now.*'

They'd usually open the full door to the kitchen which was the main living area and leave the half door closed. At that time of the morning traffic would be heavy around the farmyard with hens, ducks and geese queuing up outside the half door looking for breakfast. The geese seemed to dominate by pushing their way past the hens and ducks to get to the top of the queue. Nora would stand inside the half door throwing out hard bread soaked in milk and cold boiled spuds that were the leftovers from the previous day's dinner. Sometimes she'd have some hens indoors hatching a clutch of eggs. Other hens with their chickens would be running round the living quarters. Between the cat, the dog, the hens and chickens and the occasional mouse I think it would be fair to say that there was quite a bit of traffic indoors some mornings also. The cat and the hens had to get their breakfast but the dog would have to wait for whatever scraps Jack and Nora threw his way when eating theirs.

However, breakfast had to be cooked so it would be time for Nora to get organised after Jack finished milking. Breakfast was never a rushed occasion which was just as well. First of all the open hearth fire would have to be re-stoked and it would have to be glowing red for boiling the kettle and heating the big frying pan. From time to time Jack would throw some paraffin oil on the fire to speed things up and get it under way. Nora had a big heavy old style kettle and a big heavy cast iron frying pan which was a bit like a mini roundabout and both were usually on standby as Jack had a mighty big appetite. He could sink a pound of sausages, a few thick slices of bacon, a couple of fried eggs, onions, mushrooms and black pudding all in the same sitting. The frying pan had handles at the side and sometimes when fully loaded Nora would use a *'pothook'* (an S shaped metal hook) to lift it on and off the hot coals. It took quite a while to prime after it was placed on top of the coals on the hearth. On one occasion Jack said to Nora, 'W*e'll have to get a smaller frying pan sure Jaysus it takes about a bag of turf to heat that bloody thing up before you can start frying.'*

From time to time she'd throw a small spit on to the pan to check the temperature. If it didn't quickly evaporate she didn't consider it hot enough for O'Mara's sausages. When she considered it hot enough she'd put a big piece of lard in it and the cooking process was off to a start. The smell was appetising as Nora moved the sausages, bacon, onions, eggs and some home-made black pudding slices around the pan to prevent them from burning. The thick slices of bacon were cut off a piece that she'd take down from the rafters. It was home cured and very salty but very sweet particularly the fatty margin. The sausages tasted different from today's sausages. The spices gave them a lovely flavour so a pound of sausages didn't last Jack for very long. However, there was a bit of a problem in that, up the chimney above the frying pan there were heavy soot deposits. From time to time bits dropped down and some entered the pan to add to the mixed grill. Nora would pick out the bigger bits of soot from between the sausages and bacon. Jack would be sitting nearby observing proceedings.

One morning he said, *'Nora will you cover that bloody pan before another ball of soot hits it or sure Jaysus we won't know the soot from the black pudding slices,'* She then put a big enamel plate upside down on top of the pan. The cooking tone changed as the hot fat bounced off the plate. The kettle hanging over the fire with the water boiling at this stage had the lid bouncing up and down with the steam a bit like a train. Nora would take down a big box of loose tea from above the fireplace. Teabags hadn't hit the market at that time. She'd pour a few generous measures on to her hand and pop it in to the teapot. When everything was at the ready she'd shout, *'The breakfast is ready lads come and get it.'* The cooking process was much the same every morning except we may not have soot on the menu some mornings. Jack would get Nora to pour some of the cooking fat which he referred to as dip off the frying pan on to his plate as he liked the salty taste of the fried bacon. Despite an odd bit of soot here and there it was a great breakfast with plenty of flavour.

She liked her tea strong with plenty sugar and a good drop of milk with cream on top. Jack used to pour his tea onto the saucer allegedly to cool it but it was an old habit and something that he had been doing for years. When he'd lean forward to drink out of the saucer his long ginger grey fringe would fall forward into the saucer. One morning Nora said, *'I think we'll have to get you a bloody ribbon for your hair to keep you from washing it in the saucer every time we ate.'* Jack muttered, *'There's no danger of your hair falling into anything with all the clobber you are wearin.'* In the morning while she'd still be indoors she'd wear a hair net and some Kirby grips to keep her hair in place and it made her a bit like Ena Sharples of *'Coronation Street'*.

There were a few mice alternating between the bedrooms and the cat would run past perhaps I should say *'walk past'* from time to time in pursuit of a mouse. Sometimes the mouse would run past the cat going in the opposite direction. Jack commented, *'Nora do you know what, that bloody cat never caught a mouse. I don't know why we don't get rid of him.'* She said, *'Yerah sure what can you expect he has only one eye and arthritis in his back legs.'* He said, *'Nora, we'll need to get him a bloody white stick. Sure Jaysus a mouse would have to give himself up before that bloody cat would catch it.'* He then said, *'The auld joints in his back legs are gone a bit rusty, maybe we should throw a sup of paraffin oil on them and loosen them up a bit."* Nora would reply, *'He's been my mother's cat for years and she asked me to look after him to the end of his days.'* And Jack would say, *'Yeah, sure looking at the shape of that bloody cat I think he must have been your grandmother's as well.'* At that time mostly all the old farmhouses had a mouse or two.

They were part of the furniture.

Nora liked a good heavy spread of homemade butter on her bread. She'd always have plenty of home-made bread and butter although they'd send most of the milk to the creamery. The butter was a kind of rich golden colour. Jack sometimes preferred creamery butter. He'd say to Nora, '*Give me a bit of North Clare Creamery.*'

The dog stood nearby waiting for the bits and pieces that Jack or Nora didn't want. He'd move from one to the other snapping at anything that was thrown his way. He was a kind of mobile garbage bin. After we had that traditional type breakfast Jack became the dish washer. He'd put plates, cups, saucers, the cutlery and the frying pan all into a big basin and pour some boiling water from the kettle over them. Washing up liquid hadn't hit the market at that time so he'd throw a good couple of fistfuls of Omo, the washing powder of the day into the basin. With a good store in the belly we were ready for the day's work.

5.
Off to the Bog

Cutting the turf required a good start to the day with a good country breakfast. Once that was over preparations could begin for the road. When Jack was finished washing up it was time for him to tackle the horse to the cart while Nora put on her makeup. She had some spots on her forehead and face that required a bit of treatment. She'd apply some boiled and crushed garlic mixed with butter and Jeyes Fluid. After she applied that potent mix the smell was such that even the midges wouldn't attack her. Apparently it was some old remedy that her parents or grandparents used. Just as well that we were going out into the fresh air. She never wore lipstick or eye shadow, with the exception of being struck with a ball of soot - another type of makeup! Jack was never in a hurry and always made sure that they took plenty of grub to the bog. Turning to Nora he'd say, '*Make sure that you put plenty of grub in the bag as 'twill be a long time before we'll get back here for dinner and make sure you bring a sup of paraffin oil as well.*' The paraffin oil was to help kindle a fire when we got to the bog.

With everything ready and the dog standing in the centre of the horse cart wagging his tail, we got on our way to the bog which was a good few miles away. From time to time we'd meet neighbours that Jack was friendly with. He'd spend a bit of time chatting to them as the horse grazed along the side of the road and he'd have a few puffs of his pipe. I sat on one side and Jack on the other leading the horse. Nora was a pretty heavily built woman, around 20 stones and with a good red complexion. She sat at the back of the cart with her legs dangling. She was pretty heavy at the backend so she always had plenty to fall back on! The road leading to the bog off the main road was rough and uneven. Poor Nora was a bit susceptible to internal combustion from time to time, particularly after a chew of raw garlic and quite a few O'Mara's sausages. It caused her to belch quite a bit and it also caused her to break wind occasionally, but nothing too serious. However, there would be a couple of loud bangs as the cart bumped its way along the rugged passage leading to the bog. With her head scarf and pixie she didn't hear anything so she assumed everything had a soft landing so to speak. When we arrived at the bog the horse was un-tackled from the cart which contained a wheelbarrow, a two-pronged fork, drea and a turf-cutting tool called a sleán. Nora took care of the picnic bag that contained a bottle of black tea wrapped in one of Jack's thick socks. It was an early version of the Thermos Flask! She also had sandwiches that consisted of thick wedges of cold boiled bacon and some fried O'Mara's sausages and of course that bottle of paraffin oil to help kindle a fire. By now the garlic and sausages were beginning to really take affect and it was a race against time to find a secluded spot!

One of the first things was to kindle a fire but sometimes it would prove a bit difficult. The old turf that remained in the bog from the previous year was wet and it required the odd splash of paraffin oil from time to time to get it under way. Jack sat on the wheelbarrow and decided he'd have a smoke before starting work. It was a turn down pipe and required the usual servicing before filling it. He had a bit of fine wire that he'd run through the stem a number of times and then give it a good blow through, fill it with tobacco and light up. Finally the cutting process would start and he decided that he'd go on the drea taking the cut turf away. The drea was a flat type wooden horse drawn float which was used to take the turf away some distance from the cutting area. Nora was busy footing the turf that had been cut some couple of weeks prior. Footing turf requires a lot of bending and needless to say not very good for Nora who suffered from internal combustion. She wore a pixie to keep her head warm, wellington boots and a heavy coat. Having worked a few hours without a break Jack decided it was time for a bit of grub. Nora produced a bottle of black tea from Jack's sock, she then took some sandwiches from her picnic basket but by this time the tea was stone cold and Jack was not having any of it. 'Nora that auld tae is a bit cold.' She replied saying 'Sure God what can you expect we've been on the road all day talking to people.' After a couple of mouthfuls Jack grunted and said, 'Nora would you take the kettle and go across to that house in the distance for some water.' She set off with her black and battered kettle.

Jack collected more of the old turf to re-kindle the fire and have it ready when Nora returned. We carried on working for a while and then we had a sit down while he had a few puffs of his pipe. He didn't have a lot of teeth and the ones that he had were brown with age and heavily stained from pipe smoke and from chewing tobacco. Nora was away for quite some time and Jack was becoming a bit impatient and said, *'Jaysus, she must have gone home for the bloody water.'* Finally, Nora turned up in a bit of a distressed state. Jack asked her, *'Where the hell did you go for the water?'* She started to sob and said to him, *'Do you not see the state of me?'* On the return journey she had to negotiate a couple of hedges and fell into a large clump of briars. She was wearing thick brown stockings secured above the knee with broad black garters. They were heavy duty ones and about two inches in width. She had lost most of the water out of the kettle. She had a long gash on her thigh and scratches below the knee and the stocking on her left leg was badly torn with blood on it.

Jack had a look at her injuries and decided she required a bit of first aid. He put her in the first aid room nearby, which was the horse cart. The shafts were on top of a pile of turf to have it in a level position. He had the hand brake on which was a sod of turf at the front and back of each wheel. Jack asked me to boil a drop of water and said, *'I'll need to clane up this woman a bit.'* I had to put the kettle on the prong of the fork to hold it over the fire. He tore a strip off the lining of his jacket and wrapped it round the gash on her thigh and secured it with her black garter. He tore off another strip of lining and poured some water on it out of the kettle to clean the blood below her knee. A couple of the scratches were a bit deep so he thought of a rather clever idea. Jack didn't have a first aid kit but he always carried a Dunlop bicycle repair kit in his jacket pocket for mending bicycle punctures. So out came the Dunlop box. He took out a few patches and a small tube of solution. He applied a bit of solution around the scratches and started to secure some of the patches. Poor Nora was moaning a little but Jack didn't have a lot of sympathy for her so he turned to her and said, *'Jaysus your leg isn't going to fall off!'* The patches didn't stick very well so he ripped off another strip of lining and wrapped it over the patches to secure them. Nora didn't put the torn blood stained stocking back on. The top of the wellington boot was aggravating the scratches so Jack got his pin knife and cut off the top half of the wellington boot so poor Nora ended up with one and a half wellington boots.

With the first aid job now complete it was time for something to eat. Nora didn't feel like eating and with no water left the only alternative was to reheat the bottle of black tea in the kettle. To boil the kettle Jack stuck two bars into the ground one either side of the fire with hooks at the top like fencing pins. He had a strong wire bent S shaped to hang the kettle. Soon the kettle was steaming like a train and Nora decided to put some more dry tea in the kettle to make the black tea even stronger. She had half a pound packet of Halpin's tea and put a fistful in the kettle. She had a big lemonade bottle full of milk and an assortment of crockery to act as drinking utensils. She had packed boiled and un-boiled eggs, some cooked sausages and buttered bread, in addition to the sausages and boiled bacon sandwiches. It was not possible to boil any eggs in the absence of water. Nora had some tea only and Jack had some hard-boiled eggs and cold sausages. I had to settle for hard-boiled eggs and buttered bread.

With the picnic over Jack took out his turned down pipe and started to service it again; this time with a horseshoe nail. It wasn't going far enough into the stem but he had an alternative, Nora's hatpin stuck in the lapel of his jacket! He cleaned out the remainder of the old burned tobacco left from the previous fill and then blew through the stem to clear any new blockage. He then cut some Garryowen Plug tobacco and rubbed it in the palm of his hand, filled his pipe and lit up. He looked up at the sky and said, *'Dat's a watery lookin' sun I tink we'll get a flood.'* Nora took out a small clay pipe and asked Jack for some of the ready to use tobacco. She usually smoked Clarke's but had to make do with Garryowen Plug. She lit up and after a few puffs and a chew of raw garlic she limped back to her turf footing.

Jack and I resumed cutting the turf. It was late and the midges were getting rather vicious but they didn't seem to bother Nora due to the barrier cream that she applied that morning. A little while later she limped across to Jack and myself and asked, *'Are ye goin' to stay here all night, I need to go home and Jack* you *should be wearing your gansie at this time of the evening 'tis getting a bit cold.'* Jack's reply was; *'Ah sure I am wearing my Bawneen sure God I can't wear the two of them at the same time.'* Bawneen was a Gaelic word for a white hand knitted woollen type cardigan. She looked a bit depressed and the bandages were coming undone. He said to her, *'We'll have to tidy up your dressings a bit before we go.'* After he applied a bit more first aid he then tackled up the horse to the cart and we loaded all the tools etc. Nora sat at the front opposite side to Jack and I sat at the back. Again the rough rugged road leaving the bog caused Nora a bit of internal discomfort and there were a few loud discharges but again she didn't hear anything because of the head gear that she was wearing. However, sometime later there was a really loud bang. It would appear that she had heard it on this occasion but tried blaming Jack saying to him, *'I wish you would stop that rifting it must be the cold sausages you ate.'* Jack didn't reply. On the road back Nora was complaining about the first aid job but Jack said to her, *'You should think yourself lucky that I had the auld bicycle patches. When we get home we'll tidy you up a bit better.'* When we arrived back at the house Nora asked me to stay for dinner. She said that she cooked a hen the night before and that she'd boil some spuds. I declined the offer and headed back home on my bicycle. It was a long hard day.

The following morning I arrived early at their house ready for another day in the bog. It was much the same procedure as the previous day with breakfast before we left. The menu was a bit different with some beans and fried onions, more O'Mara's sausages and bacon, and Nora had a chew of raw garlic. I thought to myself this menu could cause Nora some problems later. She was a bit hesitant about going to the bog but Jack said, *'Look Nora why don't you come and make the tae and sure if you feel like doing a bit later on well and good.'* Her reply to him was, *'If I go to the bog today I won't be going looking for water, you know what happened to me yesterday.'* Jack filled the ten gallons creamery tank with water from a well nearby and put it in the cart. Nora asked him, *'Are we going to the creamery or the bog.'* Jack said. *'Well I'll tell you this Nora, there won't be any water shortage today.'* She was wearing the brown stocking on her right leg that she had the previous day but decided not to put on the damaged bloodstained one on her left leg. She couldn't find a pair of stockings the same colour, so she put a red stocking on her left leg and then her one and a half wellington boots. The weather was cold so she put a headscarf on outside her pixie.

We loaded up the cart and set off for the bog. When Nora saw the creamery can full of water she thought it would be a good opportunity to take some of her dirty washing with her. She loaded up an old galvanised iron bath or wash tub full of dirty washing. The procedure was similar to the day before but Nora didn't have a reaction going over the rough terrain this time. Her wounds from the previous day were still a bit sore and raw looking. She applied a bit of Jeyes Fluid to prevent infection but it stung quite a bit as it entered the deep scratches. She didn't get involved with saving the turf.

After we had some lunch she took some dirty clothes out of the old bath. She said to Jack, 'I thought when you were bringing that ten gallon tank of water I might as well make use if it as I don't feel able to go footing turf today.' She boiled a big kettle of water and got her manual washing machine in action – the wash board! It was a very windy day with good drying conditions. Jack tipped up the horse cart so that the shafts were semi vertical, tied a piece of rope to one of the semi vertical shafts and then on to a long bar that he drove into the ground some distance away. It acted as a clothesline and Nora put her washing on it but she didn't have any clothes pegs. When it was time to go home the washing was dry and Nora said to Jack, 'I didn't manage to do anything with the turf today but at least I did a bit of washing.' Toilet facilities were a bit primitive and more blushing than flushing. It was an arrangement of two stacks of turf with a strip of galvanise across the top and a couple of bits of Liscannor stone to keep it from blowing away. It could be a rather cold experience. I enjoyed my couple of weeks working with Jack and Nora and they were decent people when it came to payment.

6.
My Journey to London

In August 1954 a neighbour called Peter McMahon RIP came home from the UK on holiday. He was working as a gardener at The Beehive hotel in London. The hotel governor; Mr Chester, asked Peter to bring somebody back with him and that he would reimburse fares and any expenses. The wages would be £4.00 per week all found. It is difficult nowadays to imagine working fifty two weeks for £208.00. However, I saw it as a steppingstone to move away from Ireland and the possibility of sourcing better paid employment at some later date. My father had passed away in November 1952 so it was a difficult decision leaving my family as my brother Michael was only sixteen years old and my sister Mary fourteen while I was just still seventeen. When I told my mother that I intended leaving she was sad at the thought of breaking up the family and it would be difficult to work the land. My mother had such a difficult life as my dad was unable to work. She worked so very hard both indoors and out and, like most farmers, was dependent on credit from the local shops to buy food and other household necessities. The credit was for a short period of time - 'till the sale of cattle or a creamery cheque.

I had never been away from home before so everything was completely new to me. The night before I left my mother invited some neighbours to come round and have a little tea party and dance a few Caledonian sets. The following morning reality struck when it was time to go and head for CIE (Irish: Córas Iompar Éireann; the National Bus Company). As I started to walk downhill along the lane towards the main road I took a last look at the old home as it faded away in the distance. The river Shannon in the background was obscured with fog. My mother conveyed me about half way down the lane leading on to the main road and the bus route. She carried my little case which contained a few shirts, shaving gear, some socks and not a lot else.

When I departed I remember my mother stood in the distance and waved me a final goodbye as I boarded the bus, or as some called it *'the emigrant's daily coffin-less hearse'*. Reality really struck when the bus conductor pressed the *'go'* bell. I knew it was the final departure point as far as leaving my home and the start of a journey into the unknown. Continuing with my exit, my case was put on the roof of the CIE bus on to the baggage area. A ladder was fixed externally to the back of the bus to enable the bus conductor to access that area which was only used when the baggage well underneath the floor area and the internal roof racks were full. Every seat on the bus was taken for the first leg of the journey out of Ireland. It was such a sad occasion almost like a funeral. Some young girls were tearful and looking very distressed as the bus bumped its way along the undulating road surface. West Clare was heavily depopulated at that time, but this was true of the county as a whole and, indeed, the West of Ireland in particular.

I met my neighbour Peter on the bus and we travelled to Limerick. The next leg of the journey was the train from Limerick to Dublin, also CIE transport. We changed at Limerick Junction and then got on the Cork to Dublin train. Peter met a friend on the train and introduced me. She was from Limerick and from memory I believe her name was Bridget O'Connell. She told me that she had lived in London since the early 1940s but that every time she was home on holiday it was still very difficult going away again. She said to me, *'You'll find a big culture change when you get to London, keep your feet on the ground and never forget your home and family.'* She also said, *'Remember you're not on your own as there are thousands of Irish in London who all went there for the same reason as you and I.'* She was from a big family of four brothers and one sister who were in London, as well as a brother and sister in Limerick. I hadn't been on a train before and was pretty terrified every time the train passed under a bridge. I didn't know that there was a toilet on board and waited 'till I got to Dublin to relieve myself. Anyway I was too scared to leave my seat as I may have had problems finding it again.

Peter would say from time to time, *'It won't be long now fella.'* We duly arrived in Dublin and Peter took me along O'Connell Street to see the sights. I hadn't been in a city before and with all the tall buildings and lights I was rather stunned. I always remember spending some time watching a Donnelly sausage running from fork to fork on an overhead high wire across

O'Connell Street. The sausage was illuminated as it cart wheeled across on the wire. To me the Donnelly sausage on the wire was the equivalent of a visit to Disney Land for today's youth. The sight of a nice brown Donnelly sausage cart wheeling along the wire made me feel a bit peckish as it looked the real thing. Not sure if it is still possible to purchase Donnelly's sausages nowadays but I'm sure they wouldn't have the same appeal as the high wire trapeze sausage.

Peter took me into Clerys store in O'Connell Street. I couldn't comprehend just how big it was as we didn't have anything like it in Ennis. At that time it seemed bigger than Harrods store in London. I was overwhelmed by the merchandise on display but I didn't have money to buy anything. I thought that maybe one day, when returning home on holiday, I'd have money to buy something for my mother as she was such a good, caring, hardworking woman. Although still in Ireland, the Dublin illuminations seemed like a new world to me as electricity hadn't come to Lissycasey at that time.

After we had something to eat Peter said, *'It is time lad that we looked for a place to stay.'* On previous occasions Peter had stayed in a B&B just off O'Connell Street so we headed there. I found it difficult to settle thinking about home and not being able to talk to my family. I felt completely lost that night in the B&B. I didn't sleep very much as the traffic in O'Connell Street seemed to be going all night and everybody seemed to have a scooter which made a lot of noise. Traffic at night wasn't a problem where I was reared! Through the night I felt that I had made the wrong decision by leaving home and that perhaps I shouldn't continue. Loneliness was probably the worst thing. I think I became kind of disorientated with that feeling of uncertainty hanging over me. Even though Peter was helpful in understanding my predicament, I felt that I wanted a family member to share and discuss my decision to go to London.

On Sunday morning it was so strange to wake up in a big city without any of my family. When we went to breakfast there were a few more first time emigrants. A couple of young ladies from Kerry were seated at our table and like me they were heading to London for the first time. They too didn't sleep very much and were wondering if they had made the right decision. After Mass we set off to catch the boat train to Dun Laoghaire. Again it was packed and it was standing room only but it was only a short journey.

This was all so new to me that on a number of occasions I seriously thought about turning back, but Peter continued to reassure me that everything would be okay. The situation I found myself in was rather overwhelming for the simple reason that I found it difficult to come to terms with the big new world that I had just entered, even though I was still in Ireland. Dublin could have been Hong Kong or Moscow as nothing was familiar to me except the Donnelly's sausage. It was all so alien to me. At the time of leaving home, the extent of my travels was confined to Ennis, a distance of about ten miles. When I visited Ennis I'd always meet people that I knew but it was all strange faces in Dublin. The train journey from Limerick to Dublin, moving about the city among large crowds of people and having spent my first night away from home was just too much for me.

We finally got to the floating hearse (the boat) but before we boarded Peter took me for a cup of tea and once again tried to reassure me that I was making the right decision and that things would turn out alright for me. I couldn't help crying and tried to hide it from Peter as I did not want him to see my tears. When we boarded it was packed to capacity; some returning after their holidays and many others like me in search of a new life. It was chaos for a while as people tried to get a seat but for many it wasn't possible. I think the boat was the Princess Maude. Inside and out on the deck it was standing room only or sit on top of one's case, if it were possible to find a floor space to put it down. When the boat moved out to sea we were outside on deck and I thought I could hear cattle roaring. It seemed rather strange that it was still possible to hear cattle at that point. It was still a bit foggy but after a while it lifted and then the wind started to blow. I said to Peter, *'I can still hear cattle roaring which makes it a bit like home.'* Peter said, *'There are cattle on the boat; even Irish cattle are emigrating.'* At first I thought he was joking but the roaring continued from time to time all during the journey and it was also possible to smell them. Of course they too were getting tossed about in the rough seas.

Boats at that time were dirty with very few facilities by comparison to today's hydrofoils. As far as the shipping companies were concerned it was simply a case of packing on as many cattle and people as possible. Health and Safety didn't seem to matter. There were emigrants from different counties but mainly from the south and west. I got talking to a Sean Sullivan from Kerry who was going to London with his sister who was returning from holiday. He was only sixteen years old and he was playing an accordion. He was hoping to join a band in London where one of his brothers was already a member. He was one of a family of six. Three of his family were already living in London and two in America. Sean was a good musician and his playing raised spirits a bit on the boat. Some had other spirits raised and it wasn't by music.

At this stage of the journey the £5.00 that I left home with was down to just a few bob. I got some money from Peter to buy some food but the choice was limited and confined to cold food.

Some were overcome with grief and that was because it was no longer possible to see Ireland. It was now out of sight as it faded away into the horizon and we were getting further and further away from land. Some left sick relatives behind and others were returning after a family bereavement so for them it was an even worse situation than mine. Many had not been on a boat journey before and others were suffering from sea sickness and some were crying as the boat bounced its way over the rough sea. There were tired bodies lying all over the place. Some tried to sleep but suddenly the boat would roll from one side to the other causing people to vomit where they were sitting or lying. A small group were huddled together saying the rosary as they were terrified that the boat would sink due to the very rough seas. It got very cold out on deck but it was packed inside.

Many were thinking of their little whitewashed cottage on the hill or even down on the hollow. The little cottage and its surroundings would have been firmly fixed in the memory of many, now that the Emerald Isle was out of sight. We really were kind of refugees forced to leave our homeland through poverty and unemployment rather than war or some kind of uprising. Finally, the Holyhead Harbour lights appeared in the distance.

When we got to Holyhead everybody was rushing to catch the Irish Mail Train to London Euston and elsewhere. The Irish Mail was a big steam train that also carried the mail. Just as it was about to leave Holyhead it sounded a kind of klaxon, loud blast. For many of the emigrants on board it was a kind of a final reminder that they were about to start their journey into exile now that they were separated by water from their homeland. Again the train was packed to capacity and many had to sit on their case in the passageway for some six to eight hours. It sped across the country with smoke billowing from the big steam engine. It stopped at Crewe station in Cheshire which was a big interchange station in the northwest of England. It was parked for a long time at Crewe station as the engine had developed some kind of problem. There wasn't any heating and some elderly people were very cold and unable to sleep. There were no facilities on board to get a warm drink or something to eat and as time went by it appeared even colder. Some had a bottle of Jamieson that they shared between them and I suppose that generated a bit of internal heating. Many got off the Irish Mail at Crewe station to catch trains to other destinations such as Birmingham, Manchester and elsewhere. However it didn't solve the lack of seating as others joined the train.

Finally the steam train chugged its way out of Crewe station with big plumes of smoke billowing into the sky. As the train picked up speed the smoke changed direction and blew back over the carriages. The lights were rather dim. Many tried to sleep but the coldness of the night would wake them again as the train sped through the countryside on its journey to London. For many like me, who hadn't travelled by train before, the long journey from Holyhead in north-west Wales to London was taking its toll. Finally we arrived at London Euston tired, weary and homesick. Some had either a family member or friend waiting for them. The next leg of the journey for Peter and I was the Tube train to Gants Hill in Essex. The Tube Underground system proved to be another major challenge as it was my first experience below ground.

It was my intention to perhaps spend a couple of years or so in Britain and then return home. However, circumstances changed my intentions and as the years passed by it became more difficult to make the decision to return home permanently.

7.
First Experiences of London

Having left Ireland uneducated, people like me had to settle for whatever employment was on offer in the absence of qualifications or work experience. Many jobs were of a menial nature but anything that put a bit of money in one's pocket on a regular basis was always welcome. I was lucky on my first arrival in London because I had Peter to help me. It was, however, quite a walk from Gants Hill station to the Beehive Hotel. It was Sunday evening and when we arrived Peter introduced me to the proprietor's Mr & Mrs Chester. It was alien for me to suddenly be amongst Cockney's and for me it was a new culture, a new world that seemed a long way from home. I found it difficult to communicate with them at first and equally so they found it difficult to communicate with me. Peter kept saying, *'Never mind fella the first 100 years is always the worst.'* I went to my room and again it was a sleepless night but at this point there was no going back.

Monday morning was my first working day in the UK and for the first month or so Peter was my mentor. After breakfast I'd get a variety of jobs to do such as in the garden with Peter, packing shelves in the bar or working in the cellar. Occasionally I'd be a waiter at night and that helped to make a few extra pounds. I was introduced to Alice the cook at breakfast the first morning. She was a fair sized woman and her attitude with food was – *'you can either take it or leave it'*. The food portions were small and not the kind of food that countrymen with a big appetite's were accustomed to. Like most emigrants arriving in a big foreign city or town we missed the sights and sounds of one's home place. Sometimes small things mattered, such as friendly neighbours, or Tommy Hehir's ass roaring in the distance. The absence of things such as smells around the farmyard or views of undulating mountains or hill tops against a blue skyline with the sun shining brought memories of home flooding back and sometimes brought tears to one's eyes. It was difficult to get used to the sudden change in the daily routine.

My mother used to send me the Clare Champion newspaper every week. When it arrived at the hotel Alice used to take it to my room, knock on the door and say, *'Here is your Jewish Chronicle.'* George and his wife Nora were two of the bar staff who were friendly. At night time there was usually somebody playing a piano in the bar and they'd have a bit of a singsong but it wouldn't be the *'Wild Colonial Boy'* or the *'Stone outside Dan Murphy's Door.'* I think *'Knees up Mother Brown'* was the popular Cockney song at that time. English people liked cheese sandwiches so after the bar closed at night Alice would bring a tray of cheese and tomato sandwiches and a pot of tea into the bar for some of the staff that stayed behind. However, after a while I found most English people were friendly, but at that time some did make jokes about the Irish. It was to get a laugh and not intended to be offensive. We had our broad Irish accent with Gaelic words incorporated here and there. The Cockneys had their hammer without the letter H *'ammer'* or some *'avver bleeding fing'*.

On one occasion there was a rather funny incident concerning laundry. A local company collected the Beehive Hotel's laundry every Monday morning and returned it on the Friday. The employee's laundry was included in the collection. Being Irish Peter was always referred to as Pat and a chambermaid known as Patricia was sometimes referred to as Pat. The laundry was labelled as Pat m (male) and Pat f (female). One Friday Peter's laundry was returned but he didn't open it 'till the Saturday morning. On opening it he discovered an assortment of ladies underwear as follows: two large pair of knickers, some bras and corsets and suspenders. I think it would be fair to say that the knickers were pretty substantial. The laundry belonged to Patricia. She was a very nice lady but there was a lot of her.

Having opened the package Peter felt he was in a rather embarrassing situation so he went to see Mr Chester the proprietor to explain the mix-up. Mr Chester thought that Peter should dress up in the underwear that he got back from the laundry and have his photograph taken just for a laugh. Peter agreed and duly got changed into Patricia's underwear including the corsets etc. The knickers that he put on had heavy elasticated legs, half thigh length and were pink in colour but in these days the photos were black and white. Mr Chester had the photograph developed and put it up in the downstairs bar. The customers had a good laugh and as word spread about the photograph customer numbers considerably increased. Some customers asked Peter for his autograph and he usually obliged. When Patricia saw the photograph she was a bit embarrassed at first but then saw the funny side. She felt that the laundry mix-up had been arranged but that was not the case. Patricia had got Peter's laundry but it only consisted of shirts as Peter never wore underwear so she couldn't return the compliment. However, she thought she'd mark the occasion by giving him a little memento. She wrapped up the pink pair of knickers, some harness and the bra that Peter wore for the photo shoot and posted it to him. He saw the funny side and they both had a good laugh.

For the first few weeks I found it hard to adjust to the new way of life. Although the hotel staff were friendly it was difficult to share jokes or have a conversation that they were interested in. From memory I think that there were only about half a dozen Irish working in the hotel. We had our own dining area and our meals were at different times to the rest. I suppose it was a type of segregation. It was so different walking down the street and not knowing anybody. Nobody passed the time of day unlike the friendly people I left in my home neighbourhood. At night I'd have a stroll along the shopping area at Gants Hill. The bright lights were so different to what I was accustomed to in the dark countryside in the West of Ireland. The volume of traffic and the noise was also difficult to get used to.

I still hadn't heard from or spoken to any of my family and after the first day I knew that it wouldn't be long term in the hotel for me. I wrote to my mother and it took a couple of weeks before I got a letter back from home. I thought I'll have to stick it 'till Christmas but that was still a few months away. Since I didn't drink or smoke my only pass time was dancing. I liked dancing and ventured to the Blarney Club dancehall at Tottenham Court Road on my own as Peter's dancing days were long since over. It was about thirteen stops from Gants Hill to Tottenham Court Road, with both stations on the Central Line. The Blarney dancehall was the only one I visited for the first few weeks but then I explored a couple more. I visited The Shamrock dance hall in Elephant and

Castle and the Innisfree at Ealing Broadway. Both were owned by the Casey brothers of County Kerry. They were the famous Casey wrestlers and I believe they were world champions.

Soon after I took up my post at the Beehive Hotel, a neighbour from my home town-land Tubber was anxious to leave home and find employment in London. He was a very good friend and neighbour and I managed to secure employment for him at the Beehive Hotel. He duly arrived in London and for him it was like arriving on Mars which was exactly my experience some months earlier. When he arrived at Euston Station, London he decided to take a taxi to the hotel. The taxi driver asked him, '*Will I carry your case for you Pat?*' Then when the driver dropped him off at the hotel and got paid he said, '*Thanks a lot Pat.*' Patrick was astonished that the driver knew his name and when he got into the hotel he said to me, '*I wonder how the hell the taxi driver knew my name?*' I explained to him that all Irishmen were called '*Pat*' or '*Paddy*' in the U.K.

The weekend following his arrival we decided to go to the Blarney Club dancehall. We went to Gants Hill tube station and I got the tickets which were only a few pence at that time. I walked on to the escalator and my friend was following behind. I had forgotten to say to him to watch his step getting on to the escalator and I was nearly at the bottom when I looked behind me. My friend was lying on the flat of his back on the black belt running down the side of the Escalator but he was still getting carried downwards. Other people using the escalator were wondering what he was doing. I ran up the other side and followed him down. When he got off at the bottom he was pale and trembling and said to me, '*You are a terrible so and so for not telling me about the bloody stairs, the two feet were taken from under me.*' Afterwards we often had a good laugh about it and he saw the funny side.

London usually had periods of dense fog called smog. Occasionally, it could be really dense to the point that the street lights were ineffective. The smoke from heavy industry and steam trains couldn't vent into the atmosphere, so it fell back to the ground again and people suffering from Asthma found it difficult to breathe. The particles of black soot from the steam train engines were a real health hazard. White clothing had black deposits of soot, and when one blew one's nose onto a white handkerchief it became black also. London was an unhealthy place to be at that time. I recall a couple of bad train crashes back towards the end of the 1950s resulting in loss of life. One such train disaster was in Lewisham one year just before Christmas and I believe it was caused by dense fog.

Sometimes people were lucky as was a gentleman called Bernard Carey from Tipperary whom I worked with in Eastcote on the outskirts of London back in the late 1950s told me a nice story. He was a fine man with a wavy ginger head of hair. I believe he would be about six foot three or four inches in height and definitely a ladies man. He arrived in London penny-less in 1952 and set off walking from Euston station heading for Kilburn. He had no idea where he was going but he kept making enquiries.

When he was at home he often heard from people that had returned on holiday talking about Kilburn and all the Irish that were living there. When he arrived in Kilburn he didn't fancy going into a pub as he didn't have money to buy a drink. Neither did he have money for accommodation so he went to the Sacred Heart Church in Quex Road and explained his situation to a member of the clergy. The priest was sympathetic and gave him some money to buy a meal. He told him to call back after he had something to eat and that he may be able to fix him up with temporary accommodation.

When he returned the priest took him to one of his parishioners where he got accommodation. Bernard said that he couldn't believe his luck as it was a fine big house. He said that the first night he arrived there he put his eye on the daughter. He fell in love with her and she fell in love with him. Romance blossomed and there he remained 'till they got married in 1953. He said, 'Sure I couldn't believe my luck that I had put the ring on Rosie inside 12 months of arriving in Kilburn.' He also said that he had a bit of a problem in that the mother had an eye for him as well but as in Brendan Grace's story he said he'd prefer to marry the daughter. She was an only daughter living with her mother as her father had passed away. After they got married they had the upstairs apartment all to themselves and the mother lived on the ground floor. When the mother passed away the house was Rosie's and of course Bernard's also so he struck it lucky. They then rented out the upstairs apartment to Irish girls who worked in a biscuit factory near Cricklewood. The priest that found him the accommodation officiated at the wedding ceremony and they lived happily ever after. I heard some years later that he set up a company in London supplying labour to the construction industry. I thought it was a nice story with a happy ending and rather unique. Not very many emigrants could tell such a happy story.

8.
Returning For Christmas

When that first Christmas arrived I headed home for a couple of weeks to familiar surroundings. My return journey started at Euston where I joined the Irish Mail for Holyhead. It was quite a joyous occasion for all the returning emigrants especially when the final train whistle blew and it was on its way to Holyhead. The train was pretty full and everyone was looking forward to being at home with their families for the Christmas festivities. Most had presents for their parents and siblings. Some were playing accordions, some violins and others were singing.

The big steam train chugged its way out of London and headed out into the dark countryside with smoke billowing back over the carriages. Some slept but others were too occupied with the occasion of returning home. The train stopped at a couple of stations along the way such as Rugby and Crewe to pick up more returning emigrants. It was packed to capacity leaving Crewe but by now it was snowing rather heavily and some worried that the train wouldn't manage to get to Holyhead. When we entered Wales it was blizzard like conditions and the train was only chugging along at a very slow pace. It was late arriving at Holyhead but when we finally arrived there was a big cheer. Of course the Dublin boat couldn't sail without the train passengers.

It was a rather sad journey for an elderly gentleman called Christy Curtin returning home to Mallow, Co Cork. He hadn't made the journey home for a long number of years prior to that. He only had one brother and one sister. His brother stayed at home for a while, then sold the old home and the small farm and moved to Australia. Christy lost touch with him and the old home was gone.

Christy worked in the construction industry and suffered serious injuries when he fell off scaffolding on to a concrete floor below resulting in back and internal injuries. He spent quite some time in hospital and then lived with his sister in Hammersmith but was still attending hospital as an out-patient. He was still pretty handicapped due to a spinal injury and walked with the aid of a crutch. During his years in London both his parents had passed away but he was unable to travel to attend their funerals. He was going to spend the Christmas period with a cousin in County Kerry as he no longer had anybody in Mallow.

He was hoping that his cousin could manage to take him to Mallow as he longed to see the area where he spent his young days and Christy also felt that it would be his last journey to Ireland. The sad thing was that he was still attending a London hospital for treatment and that meant that he'd have to return, as he couldn't get that kind of treatment in Ireland at that time. He was pretty distressed throughout the journey and from time to time spoke about his young days at home with his parents and how lonely he felt that he didn't have any family in Mallow to spend Christmas with. Many had tears in their eyes and as always the generosity of the Irish abroad came to the fore. A couple of women took him along from carriage to carriage explaining his predicament and collected a considerable sum of money. He was speechless as he tried to thank everybody for their generosity. When we got to Holyhead, a couple of gentlemen helped him to get on the boat and they bought him some food. I am not sure what happened when he got to Dublin.

Again the boat journey from Holyhead to Dublin was a pretty lively occasion with people having a drink, playing music and singing. The crossing was very rough and some people were sick during the journey with rather limited facilities. It was packed to capacity and many had to sit on their cases outside in the freezing cold as they did on the outward journey.

When we arrived in Dublin it was snowing as people headed off in different directions, West, North and South. The train from Dublin to Limerick was very busy and for many there was no seating so it was a case of standing or putting down one's case on the floor and sitting on it. Everybody was in festive mood and looking forward to be reunited with family and friends. The seating situation eased somewhat after Limerick Junction when many left the train to catch connections for other destinations.

The final leg of my journey was a bus from Limerick. It was packed with emigrants heading home to West Clare. I felt so happy when I got off the bus at the bottom of our lane where my mother and sister were waiting for me. Although I was only away for a few months, it felt like a lifetime since I last saw my family. In the time I was away I had saved around £50.00. That was a lot of money in 1954 and it was the most money I ever had. I had a good couple of weeks at home and went to a few dances. I was able to give my mum some money before I went back.

Electricity hadn't come to my area at that time so at night the country was still in darkness. It was a rather strange feeling having arrived back to the quietness of the countryside from the hustle bustle of London. Although it was back to the old paraffin oil lamp and candles and the open hearth fire, it was so lovely to be back at home amongst my friends and neighbours, although I'd only been away for a short while. The smell of the turf fire and bread baking on the griddle were values that added to my homecoming.

Over the Christmas period I met many of my old neighbours at church and elsewhere. Noticeably, mostly all the youth of the neighbourhood had emigrated and any that returned for the Christmas period were mainly from the UK. For those who had migrated to America it would be too costly and time consuming to make the return journey as it took about a week to cross the Atlantic from New York to Cork. However, when the Christmas holidays finished I wasn't keen on going back to London but I knew it had to be faced or go back to where I was originally. For me leaving home again was just about as bad as when I first left and perhaps even worse for my mum. My cousin in London told me before I went home that he'd get me a job in the construction industry.

9.
Sending Money and Parcels Home

Most emigrants never forgot the struggle their parents had when they were growing up. Some worked hard for years sending most of their earnings home to help the siblings that they left behind. When I was in London I lived with many people from different counties and one of their first jobs on a Saturday morning would be to send money and a little letter home to their parents. The Irish economy benefited from the huge amounts of money many emigrants sent back home over the decades. It helped struggling families and it also helped to keep Ireland afloat. Money arrived in envelopes in different forms such as cash, money orders and postal orders. The pound Sterling and the American dollar were the two main currencies that kept bread on many Irish tables. It also helped to put new roofs on many of the old thatched houses and indeed helped with other home improvements.

The remittances sent back to Ireland were by and large spent by struggling families on day to day living. This new money entering the country helped a flagging economy which successive governments presided over. Many parents eagerly awaited a visit from the postman to hear from their loved ones and, of course, also hoping for a little bit of cash inside the envelope. It was always a bit of a lifeline to bridge the gap financially 'till the next creamery cheque or perhaps the sale of cattle or some farm produce such as butter, eggs or poultry. Most emigrants worked long hard hours and were only too happy to be in a position to help their families in Ireland. Where three or four members of a family emigrated to the UK and lived in close proximity to each other, they would club together and send money home every week while they remained single. Equally as important as money inside the envelope would be a recent photograph of their loved one.

For men that didn't have a post office savings account or bank account or family in Ireland, it was necessary to find alternative places to put their money for safe keeping. Some came to an arrangement with a member of the clergy but of course their money didn't earn any interest and most clergy expected a little bit of the savings. Others, who had family members in America would change their money from Sterling to Dollars and send it over there to be put into a bank account. Of course the reason that many men didn't have a post office savings account or bank account in the UK was that they didn't register when they came to the UK and worked under an assumed name for tax avoidance purposes. My friend Johnny RIP once told me about a Donegal man that he shared accommodation with in London. He had his girlfriend banking his money for him. She was putting the money into her account and after a period of time she closed the account and disappeared with all the money. Allegedly, he had saved in the region of £500 and that was a lot of money back in the 1950s. It was rather a sad situation to have been duped by someone that he trusted. Others depended on their landlady and in most cases there weren't any problems. However, I've heard of instances where a few landladies spent the money on bingo that they were supposed to be banking for their tenants!

Food parcels and items of clothing were also sent to help struggling family members who were too young to emigrate. American food parcels and items of clothing were always a great boost for struggling families and they had a certain magic. In some cases clothes were remodelled to fit teenagers who were too young to emigrate. Clothing from America was always welcome in our home. The smell of America off the clothing made them unique. Old suits were remodelled and I always felt special wearing them. Sheets and pillow covers had to be made from the flour bags.

Rationing in our family during World War 2 sometimes resulted in shortages of food particularly flour. My mother did the best she could trying to eke out a living from the meagre rations and my family were somewhat fortunate to have a caring aunt and uncle; Mick and Bridget who emigrated to America in 1906 and 1908 respectively. From time to time they sent us flour, clothing, tea, candy and other bits and pieces. My uncle Mick sent us ten stone bags of flour at pretty regular intervals during the war years when rationing was in place. That was one of the most important things to help keep bread on the table. The flour was snow white and very fine. My mother mixed it with Indian meal in an effort to make it last for as long as possible. The Indian meal was yellow in colour and very coarse. It was intended to be for animal feed. It made the bread very hard and unpalatable.

On one occasion a bag of flour arrived at the Post Office in Lissycasey but our address was either torn off or not legible. Luckily my uncle's name and address were still intact so it was returned to him. He readdressed it and sent it on its way once again and it arrived back some three plus months later having travelled around the world. It had all the ports of call stamped on it. It was estimated to have travelled in excess of ten thousand miles which was perhaps one of the most travelled bags of flour in the world. He also sent clothing and our aunt Bridget sent tea, currants, raisins and candy etc. I always remember the boxes of tea with *'CEYLON TEA'* written on them - semi vertical bottom to top. I also remember something else that was written on the boxes, *'Never use water that has been boiling for a long time.'*

At that time parents struggled to put food on the table for their children and in some cases it was a bit like the miracle of the loaves and fishes. Farming communities were dependent on the sale of cattle and some farm produce such as eggs, butter, turf and bog dale to generate a bit of income; but the bit of income generated wasn't nearly enough to provide for a large family. Some were more fortunate in that they were more or less self-sufficient so far as food was concerned. They'd have milk, eggs, butter, potatoes, bread and meat such as pork and chicken; but of course there were many that didn't have these provisions. Even those who had good provisions still faced periods of shortages. For example in winter cows were dry, which meant restricted amounts of milk and no home produced butter, therefore no buttermilk for baking bread. Eggs would also be in short supply. Some years the potato crop might fail due to a mid summer frost or blight in late July or August at the height of the growing season. This was a problem in some cases in that the spuds were one of the main dishes at dinnertime to satisfy a large hungry family.

For many households overcrowding was a problem particularly for large mixed families, in that cottages were small and lacked basic amenities. It was stressful for teenagers and it had a profound effect on many parents watching their sons and daughters growing up with little prospects of finding employment and knowing that emigration would inevitably be the outcome. When a sibling left home it was a fracture in the family bond and as more and more siblings left the fracture got bigger and bigger. For the one's that didn't return it meant loss of contact with friends in the neighbourhood where they were reared.

Hunger, cold and depression took its toll on many young people and some suffered ill health as a result of the austere 1940s. Young people didn't have transport to travel away from home to seek employment and even if they did there was no employment. Communication was another problem in that households didn't have a telephone and of course mobile phones weren't even invented. I can only recall two telephones in the parish of Lissycasey then and they were at the Post Office and The Police Station. The youth of rural Ireland back in the '40s and '50s grew up in a dark world by comparison to today's youth so far as communication was concerned.

The Emerald Isle of the above era was fragmented. There was the north-south divide and in terms of wealth it was an east-west divide. In the west, farm acreages were small and a lot of the land non productive by comparison to the east and mid east. At that time the agricultural industry provided only an existence particularly for the people along the western seaboard. Growing crops or rearing cattle were on a small scale. The income generated such as the sale of cattle and farm produce would only amount to about a £1000 annually for the bigger farmer and much less for the smaller one. Manufacturing and construction were almost non-existent with the odd exception and this was pretty well the case throughout rural Ireland, but particularly in the west. There was a bit of construction work every spring-time in my area, but it was mostly crows and magpies building nests on trees! There were a limited number of jobs in the Civil Service for those who were fortunate enough to have been educated.

10.
Exploiting Tax Loopholes

The numbers entering Britain may have been higher than previously stated in that it is unlikely that the records took account of the many people that didn't register for a National Insurance Number or have a tax code with the United Kingdom Inland Revenue. Many Irishmen entering Britain at that time didn't register for at least two reasons. One was to avoid being conscripted into the British Army to do National Service and the other was income tax evasion. The reason that Irishmen were reluctant to do National Service was that when they left home their endeavour was to get cash to assist their parents or other family members whom they had left behind. As many Irishmen often said, *'We left home to find work, not to fight.'*

In the 1950s and 1960s thousands of Irishmen were working in Britain in the construction and utilities industries under assumed names for sub contractors. Many sub contractors were allegedly taking care of tax and insurance payments on behalf of their employees but in a number of cases that didn't happen. Young single Irishmen got on the boat in Dublin and off at Holyhead and as many didn't register and get a National Insurance number when they entered Britain, it is unlikely that they became emigrant statistics. Some did even better in that they did get a National Insurance number and an income tax code but they'd allege to be somebody else.

Here is how it worked, they'd come to an arrangement with somebody about their own age in their neighbourhood in Ireland who had a large family and get their marriage certificate and the birth certificates of all the children. The person who made the documentation available would be a farmer unlikely to require it but should the paperwork be required it was only a matter of putting it in the post back to Ireland. He may get thirty or forty pounds annually from the recipient. The farmer would collect the Child Benefit as usual in Ireland. The recipient would return to Britain armed with the necessary documentation to secure a very good income tax code meaning that he'd pay little or no income tax due to the large number of dependants. He too would collect the Child Benefit in Britain although he didn't have a wife or family. Of course if he didn't collect the Child Benefit it would look rather suspicious.

The Child Benefit was more generous in Britain than Ireland at that time so it was a nice little earner but the deception didn't stop there. The person in Ireland that made the documentation available stamped his card in Ireland until he had the requisite number of stamps to qualify for the Irish State Pension which I believe was 156 contributions or approximately three years worth of stamps. When he qualified to draw the State Pension he'd also have allegedly worked in Britain for perhaps some ten or even up to twenty years although he never left Ireland making him eligible for the British State Pension so he ended up with two State pensions! The shadow (or recipient) would also stamp his Irish card to ensure that he also qualified for the Irish State Pension. That entire scenario fell apart with the introduction of computers and greater co-operation between the British and Irish governments and it couldn't happen nowadays. It is unlikely that the Irish authorities were aware of all the movements of people in and out of Britain for the above reasons and particularly where aliases were used.

There were other emigrants who did register in their own name, but worked with sub-contractors on what was termed shift work or the lump. They worked on aliases and were paid by the shift but didn't pay income tax or National Insurance. They signed each week on their own name as being unemployed and collected unemployment benefit. There were lots of combinations used to avoid the tax man. Some men would work in their own insurance card and authentic tax code for a number of months. They'd then sign on as unemployed and collect unemployment benefit but continue to work with a sub-contractor on a shift-work basis without any income tax or insurance stoppages. They'd then go back working on their insurance card again after it had a rest and of course they'd get a tax rebate.

There was yet another way of collecting money back in the 1950s and that was by signing on as unemployed but signing with different names in different parts of London, Birmingham or some other big city. Sometimes they'd sign in Gaelic or simply put an

X instead of a signature and then after a period of collecting unemployment benefit in a city they'd move to another city for another period. Of course tax avoidance similar to the ones detailed above was operated by other nationalities also.

There was another tax avoidance dodge. Back in the 1950s and into the 1960s it was possible to buy sets of cards (National Insurance and Income Tax Codes) in pubs or perhaps from somebody moving away from Britain. Sets of cards and the relevant documentation could be purchased for about £50 or less in some cases. Although that was a lot of money in the 1950 it would be a good investment in terms of the revenue generated over a period of a few years in relation to the small amounts of tax paid and the unemployment benefit collected. In some cases cards were sold on again. Some would purchase a couple of sets of cards but of course they would be in different names. Here is how it worked - they'd work for short periods on each set of cards and then leave that employment and sign on as being unemployed. They'd go to work on another set of cards whilst collecting unemployment on the original set. After a few months they'd pack up their job yet again and return to work using the original set of cards and of course they'd then get a tax rebate. They'd continue to alternate the sets of cards. With the tax rebates, the unemployment benefit (perhaps multiplied by two) and the wages from their legitimate employment (their own cards) it was a nice little earner. Some single Irish women also used tax avoidance methods the same as their male counterparts. They'd purchase sets of insurance cards with documentation such as a marriage certificate and maybe half a dozen children's birth certificates.

Muck - deleterious soil - shifting and the supply of materials were other areas where a few bob could be made. On the muck shifting there were a couple of ways to enhance the weekly earnings. Some drivers were self-employed and they'd agree a rate per load to shift muck from big construction sites. They'd fly tip a number of loads which meant that the fly tipped muck didn't cost them anything so far as tipping charges were concerned. They'd get paid for the loads that they fly tipped by presenting tip tickets supplied by a weighbridge operator with whom they had an arrangement. Another means of making a few bob was to come to an arrangement with a weighbridge operator who'd issue tickets for ghost loads - loads that weren't tipped -and the driver would sign the tickets. The loads were charged on a tonnage basis. The tip owners got paid for loads that weren't tipped by invoicing the company that the driver represented and had signed tickets on their behalf. Another trick was to enhance the weight value of loads meaning that the tonnage on the signed tickets were greater than what was actually tipped. Again the driver would sign the tickets to authenticate them. That also applied to the supply of materials where the weight values on the tickets would be enhanced and the driver got a daily or weekly payment from the supplier of the materials. Ah yes, if there was a loop hole or a way to make a few extra pounds it was fully exploited.

Working under fictitious names really wasn't worth the risk in that if earnings were declared it wouldn't attract very much by way of tax deductions particularly those who only worked a few days per week. Working under a fictitious name or any other tax avoidance method might well put a bit more money in one's pocket short term. However, later in life it meant a considerably reduced state pension and the loss of other benefits such as unemployment benefit, holiday pay, or sickness benefit. Over the years particularly in the 1950s and '60s many Irishmen were injured, some seriously and there were many fatalities. For major injuries they couldn't claim compensation for loss of earnings or unemployment benefit and in some cases were obliged to pay for any hospital treatment. Sometimes when a hospital visit to A&E was necessary due to an accident at work some would use a friend's name that was registered and paying tax and national insurance contributions. Young Irishmen arriving in Britain and registering had the problem of being conscripted into the British Army to do their National Service. I believe National Service finished about 1960. A lot of Irishmen continued working incognito right through the 1960s but a lot of companies who employed them ended up in court in the late '60s and early 1970s. Of course by that time many companies had accrued large amounts of cash over a period of twenty plus years of exploitation of their fellow countrymen. Of course the methods of tax avoidance described above were largely confined to the construction and utilities industries and in no way applied to all Irish sub-contractors or employees throughout the industries as a whole.

11.
Payment Methods

The majority of people leaving Ireland in the 1950s headed for Britain particularly from the west and south where the fog of unemployment hung heaviest. It was a short hop across the pond. Other routes out of Ireland by sea to Britain were Rosslare to Fishguard, Dublin to Glasgow and Derry (Londonderry) to Glasgow. Despite all the criticism of Britain down through the years the southern Irish were fortunate to be able to access the UK unrestricted and source employment back in that era. They had the same entitlement to benefits and the Health Service as UK citizens. I am not sure that all Irish emigrants were appreciative of having the UK on their doorstep as an escape route. Emigrants arriving in the UK weren't processed such as emigrants arriving in America at Ellis Island. This is based on my own experience.

Irish citizens arriving in Britain were seen as being beneficial to the State rather than being a burden. They were prepared to work hard and in the 1950s their services were in demand particularly in the construction and utilities industries as well as hospitals and factories. The British government weren't being selective by restricting Irish entry to skilled labour only. Many Irishmen went to night classes in London and elsewhere to learn bricklaying, joinery and other trades. Skilled or unskilled men and women alike were allowed entry to Britain. Had Britain closed the door on the Irish or restricted the numbers entering back in the 1950s then Ireland would be in an even worse state. It was a time when up to seventy-five per cent, three in every four people leaving Ireland headed for Britain, mostly unskilled and many with a poor education. The bombing of Britain during the Second World War by the Germans created a lot of employment particularly in the construction industry. London in particular was rebuilding a lot of damaged properties in addition to other major construction projects. Of course there was a lot of demolition work of bombed buildings also in progress.

Working in the construction industry in the UK was rough and heavy but better paid than factory work and had some advantages. For some it was easier for tax avoidance as they moved about from sub-contractor to sub-contractor using aliases. At that time pubs were a bit like job centres, particularly at the weekend. Some of the more famous pubs for obtaining employment and collecting payment in the London area were in Camden Town, Harlesden, Cricklewood, Hammersmith, Willesden, Kilburn and a few other places. Mostly all were either Irish managed or Irish staffed pubs and would be packed by day and night at the weekends during opening hours.

They were somewhat unhealthy places for both customers and staff. Just about everybody smoked at that time and bars and lounges would have dense clouds of blue smoke. People weren't aware of the dangers of passive smoking as smoking laws and regulations hadn't been introduced. Pubs in the above areas were always busy places at weekends where the craic could be enjoyed. Some were frequented by sub-contractors to recruit men and pay wages. Both the pub landlords and sub-contractors benefited from this in that it considerably increased business for the landlords provided free office accommodation for the sub-contractor's. I saw contractors paying men by producing a wad of notes and counting out the due amount. On some occasions some men wouldn't know if they were paid the correct amount or otherwise. Some contractors deducted money for transport to and from site also for insurance and tax that they were allegedly handing over to Her Majesty's Government. So with subs and the other deductions that I've mentioned some men wouldn't have any idea what exactly their wage should be. It was all the more difficult when contractors didn't give a pay slip. It would be a brown envelope with just a name written on the outside.

In the event of arguments over amounts due, some contractors would blame their wages clerk and give an assurance that the discrepancy would be rectified the following week, but on occasions the shortages continued. Over a number of weeks the on-going aggregate in payment discrepancies would get so confused that the employee would eventually lose out. Of course it was just another ploy by contractors to short pay men from week to week in the knowledge they couldn't walk away while being owed money. However, it would be difficult for any of these men to take legal action to recover the money owed for obvious reasons. First of all they were working incognito to avoid paying income tax and secondly they didn't have any detailed payslips showing the rate per shift and the number of shifts worked each week. The only course of action available would be to take it out of the contractor's nose meaning to beat him up and force him to pay. The system of payment used by many sub- contractors meant that they could offer competitive rates when tendering for work and they wouldn't have to pay office staff and associated office costs. They didn't have to worry too much about Her Majesty's Revenue and Customs (HMRC) tax returns.

It was dangerous for the contractor to have large sums of money either loose or in brown envelopes but some had minders. A subcontractor that frequented a pub in Cricklewood didn't always pay men the money that they were due. One Saturday afternoon when he was in the process of paying wages a number of angry men that were short paid some weeks earlier set about him and took the money that he was carrying. They divided it out among themselves although at that time they were employed elsewhere. A fight erupted and his minder got hurt. The police were called but by the time they arrived the contractor had left the pub. He didn't take any action against the men as he was a brown envelope man and had a bit of baggage relating to tax avoidance.

It didn't matter too much to some men how they were paid as it would be quickly deposited in the pub buying drink immediately after they got their money. A Pole once said, '*Paddy keep pay packet and throw away money but Pole keep money and throw away pay packet.*'

Some men would have only a small amount of money due to them as they would have subbed a big portion of their wage through the working week and in some cases they'd only work a few days a week. Many men would leave the pub penny-less at closing time as they would have spent their wages on drink and cigarettes. Some would have to get a sub from the contractor before they left the pub. By Monday morning that sub would also be in the possession of the pub landlord and it would be empty pockets and sore heads for some to start the week. That meant another sub at the start of the working week to get some grub on site and the entrance fee in the evening. The '*entrance fee*' was having enough money to buy the first pint at the start of the evening drinking session. Thereafter, they'd hope that their friends would buy them a drink at the start of their pub shift. If that failed, they'd have to resort to getting drink on the slate - getting it on credit.

12.
Headings and the Square Mouth Shovel

nowy Kennedy, Chambers, De Lacy, Kelly brothers and
Kennedy brothers were some of the prominent sub-
contractors back in the 1950s who usually recruited labour
for out of town work in the pubs on a Saturday or a Sunday
afternoon. A lot of the work was laying gas and water mains as
well as telephone and electric cables or excavating holes for
electricity pylons at various locations out of London. Most
contractors paid good wages but the work was rough and in some
cases short term.

Sometimes the pub was a good place to socialise, meet friends,
discuss work and even demonstrate how it should be done. Men
working in headings, which was a type of tunnel liked to
demonstrate how headings should be timbered or shored. The
timber men or *shuttering joiners'* loved to show off this skill. To
do this the requisite items were an un-sliced loaf of bread, box of
matches, scissors, some strips of cardboard and glue. First of all
the inside of the loaf had to be hollowed out to form the heading.
Then some matches were glued together to act as side trees and
head trees. Next little strips of cardboard were cut to act as
sideboards and headboards and flooring. It was a rather delicate
operation but looked like a work of art when finished. Sometimes
more work was done in the pub at night than on site during the day.
By the time the heading job was complete most were feeling merry
and arguments could arise about the correct method of timbering a
heading. It could sometimes go to battle to resolve the issue as
closing time approached. However, as they would say, '*The craic
was good.*'

In the real world heading dimensions were approximately three
feet in height and two feet to two feet six inches in width. Candles
were used for lighting where a power supply wasn't available. The
candles would be stuck between two nails on a side tree and when
the wood started to smoulder in such a confined space it brought
tears to one's eyes. I worked with some rough men and in some
rough working conditions. Sometimes ground conditions were such

that water was a problem as there was a constant drip onto one's back and of course it made the heading slippery and wet. On some occasions the excavated material had to be taken out to the shaft in bags so one can appreciate the terrible conditions in which this work was carried out. It was dangerous and backbreaking work as it was mostly a kneeling job due to the dimensions of the workspace but usually paid well. Some men worked in headings for years and because of the cramped working conditions many suffered from back problems as well as rheumatism and arthritis. I worked in headings for only a few short periods as I was a bit claustrophobic. This was due to being trapped for a short period in a heading at Cromwell Road, Knightsbridge London after a small ground collapse. I only had a few scrapes but was otherwise unhurt. Where pneumatic drills had to be used noise and dust became hazardous in such confined spaces. Timbering a heading was a very skilled operation and a good timber-man, shuttering joiner, could command a better rate of pay than the men on the labouring side of the job.

Joe Garvey RIP a Cork man was a very good timber-man and a really nice person whom I had the pleasure of working with on a few occasions. I worked with him on a job near Shepherds Bush. It was a heading for an eighteen way ducting or conduit for post office cables. It was payment per foot going forward to include timbering. It was possible to earn £30 plus per week and that was very good money back in the 1950s. It was about three feet wide and three and a half feet in height so it was a kneeling job but without prayer! After the ducting was laid, it was necessary to pack the heading with concrete. The heat of the concrete when it was setting made working conditions inside the heading almost unbearable because we were in very cramped conditions. The concrete had to be relayed by shovel from one man to the next and ultimately to the packer.

At a lunch break one day a member of the team, big Martin, a Kerryman, didn't have a knife to cut a loaf of bread, but he wouldn't be beaten. He asked Joe Garvey for his handsaw, which he used for cutting timber. He cleaned it by rubbing it across his jacket a couple of times and then sliced the whole loaf into very thick slices. He then said, '*What's wrong with that lads, sure 'tis better with good thick slices.'* He knew that some Englishmen were looking on and tried to impress. He fried a pound of steak in a square mouth shovel and scoffed the lot, including the bread. The English Engineer on site that day said that he'd seen many things before by way of improvisation but he never saw a loaf of bread cut with a handsaw for cutting timber.

On that job Martin wasn't the only one to fry steak on a square mouth shovel. Many Irishmen relied too much on the frying pan. For many the rough lifestyle had a detrimental effect on their health in later years. Due to the nature of their employment and accommodation, meals were irregular and sometimes poorly cooked and combined with the Woodbine and Arthur Guinness products it certainly could be described as an unhealthy lifestyle. On occasions it was necessary to eat one's meals out in the open in rain, frost or snow. Most Irishmen weren't registered with a doctor for obvious reasons and because of this they didn't have any regular health checks for blood pressure, cholesterol and other health problems. Excessive use of alcohol and foods with high fat content resulted in strokes and heart attacks and a premature end to their working lives. That was about 1957 or 1958, but I can still visualise the square mouth shovel on a gas ring with a pound of steak frying on it.

13.
Contractors

Many Irish people formed their own company, such as John Murphy, McNicholas Construction, M.J. Clancy from Caherea, County Clare, Lowry and MJ Gleeson to name but a few. John Murphy, McNicholas Construction and Lowry carried out some very large utility contracts throughout the UK. MJ Gleeson also another big construction company had many large contracts throughout the UK. I believe Mr Gleeson was a native of Galway although some thought County Clare. They employed a lot of Irish men and usually paid well. They would also have a very good on site accommodation for drying clothes and took the welfare of their employees seriously.

All these companies employed a lot of Irish labour, particularly John Murphy who had some large contracts in the utilities industry. They collected men each day from various parts of London particularly Camden Town as well as other locations also, for out of London contracts. Many were paid by the shift and may only work a few days per week.

Many Irishmen remained loyal employees of John Murphy and worked hard to retain their reputation. A lot of Kerry men were employed by this company that were very good workers and were well paid. John and his brother Joe were from Cahirciveen, County Kerry and they set up in business in the late 1940s. They were known as the Green and the Grey.

I recall John Murphy arriving at Cromwell Road, London. It was one of his sites where the installation of an eighteen way Post Office ducting was in progress. He was well dressed and wearing a tie. A section of deep excavation had collapsed and one employee had been trapped for a short period. When John arrived, work was in progress shoring up the excavation. John quickly removed his tie and jumped into the excavation in his good suit. He assisted with the shuttering operation and then took away the employee who had been seated in the van recovering. He took him back to his accommodation and told him to have the rest of the week off on full pay. Although John liked his *pound of flesh* he was a decent man and never expected his employees to do something that he couldn't do.

In the early days, his contracts were mostly cable work and that was very labour intensive particularly for the days of the big pull. Some prominent employee names that I recall were 'Elephant' John O'Donoghue, Concrete Sullivan, Con Hartnett, Mossy Riordan and a few others. Not sure how some got these titles but they were all great men. Perhaps their titles were associated with strength or they were specialists at some task in their field of work. I believe John O'Donoghue got the 'Elephant' title because he lived in Elephant and Castle. Regardless, of the company that one worked for on utility or construction, in relation to current pay and conditions, I think it was a type of slave labour when one considers site conditions, rates of pay and the number of hours worked per day.

In the 1950s there were some major construction sites in London particularly around the city centre. The work was carried out mainly by companies such as Sir Robert McAlpine, (McAlpine Fusiliers), John Laing and George Wimpey to name but a few. Thousands of Irishmen were employed by these companies. Some interpreted the spelling of Wimpey as '*W*E *I*NJURE *M*ORE *P*ADDIES *E*VERY *Y*EAR – OR—*W*E *I*MPORT *M*ORE *P*ADDIES *E*VERY *Y*EAR'! Of course neither was the case and these interpretations were only for a bit of fun. Having worked for Wimpey for a while in London I found it to be a good company but it was no place for slackers. They'd have a big man patrolling the site all day and some used to call him the Crucifier. He'd soon weed out any man that didn't have his head down and his arse up. However, Wimpey valued most of their Irish employees and some worked for them for up to 40 years. A lot of Irishmen liked to say I'm working for George (Wimpey) driving a mixer, or rough shuttering or a banks-man but not very often as a labourer. Doing one of the above jobs meant getting a few pence per hour more than labouring. Of course like most other companies Wimpey got their money's worth and a bit more out of Paddy.

Some sub-contractors in the Harlesden area used some of the local pubs at weekends as their offices to carry out business. I believe a couple of the contractor's were Kerry men and they were nice people. I was employed by one of them for a period of time out around Bushey on Oxon area near Watford. He was a decent sub-contractor and always paid me the agreed amount.

Wheathampstead a village in St Albans was also another area that I worked in and taking into consideration the hours on site and travelling time it was approximately a 12 to 13 hour day. This employment was for another contractor. I believe it might have been for a Wembley company; not sure if it was Circle Construction Direct or a contractor that had taken the work from that company. The work was excavating footings or foundations for houses, garages and walls, concreting and drainage work for large housing estates. Some workmates that I recall were Tim Joy, Jim O'Shea, Christy Callahan and Morris Sullivan all from Kerry. They were all lovely people trying to earn a crust in difficult circumstances.

Michael Clancy set up his own company towards the end of the 1950s. Originally he had a small office in Wembley High Road. At that time I lived nearby at St. John's Road. I knew Michael before he emigrated as he was from the next town land called Caherea. I also knew his brothers Tommy and Paddy and his wife Kathleen Kelly who came from Lissycasey. I recall visiting his Wembley High Road office when I lived nearby in St. John's Road, seeking employment, but his sites were located some distance away and travelling would be a problem for me as I didn't have my own transport. On occasions I used to meet Michael at St. Joseph's RC Church in Wembley High Road. This church was also attended by the great boxer Henry Cooper but I don't think Michael and Henry had anything in common so far as their professional lives were concerned. He moved to Harefield, cleared an old site, demolished some old buildings and built new offices there. It is quite an impressive place and he named the offices Clare House. He transported Liscannor Stone from County Clare and that considerably enhanced the stonework. He built up a reliable and skilled workforce. Sometime later the name changed to Clancy Docwra and now they are a group of companies but still privately owned. He secured some big contracts with big utility companies throughout the UK. He always treated his men well and was generous with payment. He became one of the great established Irish companies in Britain that has stood the test of time. Yes,

Michael Clancy the man from Caherea was a good ambassador for County Clare.

Some of the bigger companies such as Wimpey and a couple of others would help their employees save money on a weekly basis. The company would deduct an agreed amount from an employee's wages, if he wished to avail of that arrangement. It helped employees when they were making a claim for means tested benefits in that they didn't declare any savings made through the arrangement with their employer.

Some companies had gangers who were big rough men. Many of these men wished to have the name of being hard men and some liked the title of *'horse this'* or *'horse that'*. They'd abuse and exploit young Irish lads who had only arrived in the UK and weren't familiar with working in the construction or utilities industries. Perhaps I should make it clear that most ganger men were considerate towards young men who were endeavouring to learn the ropes as it were. Most young men were willing to work hard but required a bit of help and encouragement to gain the necessary experience. Men congregated in the mornings at various pickup points in London looking for what they called 'the start'.

Each company had their own pickup points and they would have recruiting agents there to select the men that they required. Camden Town seemed to be one of the main pickup points for the big companies such as Murphy, McNicholas, Lowry and Kennedy Brothers. They'd quickly select the number of men required for the work. They went for the big brawny lean looking men as a first option. Anybody wearing wellington boots turned down at the top with a good bit of hardened concrete around the toe caps and carrying a donkey jacket and *'foot iron'* almost certainly got a job. The *'foot iron'* was a very important piece of technology or a kind of navvy symbol or passport to obtaining employment. Anybody wearing *'Yorks'* and carrying a foot iron were deemed to be a kind of *'time served navvy'* or 'twas a kind of university degree for the construction and utilities industries. Incidentally a *'foot iron'* was a flat steel type plate to protect the sole of the shoe when digging with a shovel or graft, and *'Yorks'* were usually corduroy trousers tied below the knees, is the best way I can describe them, and they were probably made in Yorkshire. Some would have a little bag of sandwiches.

The so called gimp, (we often heard the expression *'look at the gimp of him'*) was a determining factor by which agents selected men for employment. Gimp was a kind of slang word for men with a certain posture or body position. When a man was selected for employment he would be told to jump on a particular wagon. He wouldn't have any idea of the site location or the time it took to travel there. It would be a kind of mystery tour. Sometimes when men asked where the job was, they'd be told, *'Just jump on the wagon and the driver will take you there.'* It would sometimes be a terrible experience for young lads arriving on a site after a long journey out of London wet and hungry. They'd be told, *'Jump into that trench and grab hold of that so and so cable and pull it along the bottom.'* If they asked any questions they might get a string of four letter words. Some young lads maybe sixteen or seventeen years old wouldn't have the proper clothing or footwear and within half an hour they'd be even wetter and hungrier than when they arrived on site. They wouldn't have money for grub but some of their work colleagues who were kind and considerate would take them to a café and buy them a meal. They wouldn't ask for a sub perhaps because they wouldn't know anything about subbing or perhaps they'd feel too ashamed. In the evening they would have to travel back to London wearing the same clothing, soaking wet which they had worked in all day. Some wouldn't come back the following day often regretting that they ever left home. They'd feel too ashamed to admit failure and they wouldn't want their parents to know of their dilemma.

It was indeed very sad to see young, soft, red-faced Irish lads standing in Camden Town, Kilburn or elsewhere, cold and wet, in the early hours of the morning hoping to get a job. At six o'clock in the morning it would be very unlikely that any of these young men would have had a breakfast or even a cup of tea. More often than not they'd have to return to their accommodation cold wet and hungry and wait for another day. Some wagons were open back in that they didn't have a canopy or shelter. On occasions tipper wagons would have remnants of wet muck stuck to the floor and sides from the previous day's work. One can only imagine jumping on that type of transport at 6.30 am to get to work.

A friend of mine who travelled on open back wagons told me that on a number of occasions they'd travel out of London for up to two hours. Sometimes it would be raining for the whole journey and the men would huddle together under a tarpaulin. Eventually the floor of the wagon would become water logged. They'd arrive on site wet, even before they started work, and jump into an excavation full of water or start pulling cable with a big *'Westie'* shouting orders. A *'Westie'* would be a big Mayo, Galway or Kerry man. It may be midday before they got a break or some six hours after they left Camden Town and perhaps by that time wet to the skin but as big Tommy Patten used to say, *'Sure 'tis bad skin lads that wouldn't keep it out.'*

For cable pulling additional labour would be required during the days of what was called *'the big pull'*. *'The big pull'* would be pulling thirty three thousand volt cables by hand, usually over a considerable distance. The trench would have been hand excavated by men, who were almost the equivalent of today's mini excavators, over a number of days prior to *'the big pull'*. The trench might be water-logged in places but an assortment of Irish water pumping systems would quickly spring into action. They'd range from old safety helmets to old wellington boots with the tops cut off, or old pails, or perhaps it would be an old saucepan for boiling eggs without the handle. They were easy to move about and worked instantly in clean or dirty water and didn't require priming or fuel. The assortment of manual operated pumps all working in harmony would quickly dispose of the pockets of water from the trench.

Yes, improvisation was the name of the game or where there's a will there is a way but Irishmen wouldn't be beaten! Pulling thirty three thousand volt cables was dirty, heavy work and extremely cold because the handling of the cable was mostly carried out without gloves. In frosty weather conditions the cable stuck to one's hands, sometimes removing bits of skin. The big cable drums were jacked up and the cable pulled directly off the drum. They would either be Pirelli or British Insulated Calendar's Cables (BICC). It was a team effort and the foreman/ganger shouted the orders. It was a bit like a tug of war except everybody was pulling in the same direction. I recall working in south Wales back in the late 1950s on a cable contract. To ensure that the team all pulled in harmony and at the same time the ganger kept shouting at regular intervals, *'HI- HUP HI- HUP'* and *'Pull up on the slack lads'*. There would be some men in the bottom of an excavation sometimes with water up to the top of their wellington boots threading the cable under existing services, and in between the *'HI HUP'* and *'Pull up on the slack lads'*, there would be a string of four letter words and none of them would be Holy Mary or Amen. In many cases men worked long hours without a break and were cold, dirty and wet.

Some young lads would be terrified of the big rough gangers shouting and swearing and the work seemed to be so difficult for them. Some gangers didn't want men from certain counties and that would quickly become apparent after men were only on site a couple of days. I witnessed young lads walking away in tears from some of these cable jobs following just a few hours work. They didn't get any payment but a torrent of abuse shouted at them by an idiot of a ganger man as they left the site. In most cases they wouldn't have any money to get them back to London or some other city or town.

In one particular job just outside Port Talbot I saw two lads walk off a site one day just before lunchtime and it was their first day on the job. The ganger responsible for their departure was set upon by some of their colleagues and he was badly beaten. Allegedly he was a man with a bit of a reputation who liked to bully young lads who weren't familiar with working on cable or construction jobs. The young lads were returned to site by their colleagues and the ganger man was taken away to hospital. He didn't return to site but the job continued that day and a replacement ganger took over the next day.

It was suspected that the contractor was claiming and getting paid subsistence allowance for all the men working on that contract because they had travelled from London and were living either in rented accommodation or full board and lodging. It was an arrangement between the contractor and company personnel on-site. They had an equal share. The down side was that the men didn't get any subsistence allowance. That is just another example of how some Irish contractor's exploited their countrymen and quickly accumulated wealth back in the 1950s.

Not everybody would be suitably dressed for the rough site conditions. Some of the part timers (two or three days a week lads) would be wearing Hush Puppies or Winkle Pickers when Hob Nail boots or Wellington's would be more appropriate. Nowadays, winches are used for cable pulling so the big lorry loads of men for that task are no longer required. The men were transported in wagons but only some had canopies mounted on the back. The seating in the canopies were planks of wood that were somewhat uncomfortable for long journeys. As the years went by, that type of transportation for men became illegal for safety reasons. On arrival on-site the canopies became changing rooms.

14.
1 RB Paddy and Living on Site

Basic labouring in the construction and utilities industries was completely alien to a lot of young Irishmen who came from farming communities. For many, including me, entering large construction or utility sites in London or other cities or towns could be an eye opening experience. Initially, safety was an issue in that most young Irishmen didn't have previous experience of working in hazardous construction sites or the utilities industries. On many occasions this resulted in serious injury and some were fatal. It was a different way of life to working in agriculture. Induction courses concerning safety prior to commencement of work on- site were unheard of at that time. Protective clothing and equipment were not issued and any bits of protective clothing that might be issued wouldn't be worn. For many Irishmen, safety helmets were white handkerchiefs knotted at each corner and mainly used to keep their hair clean, but didn't offer a lot of protection from bricks falling on one's head.

The knotted white handkerchief type of safety helmet was used when working with pneumatic drills or 'Paddy's motorbike' particularly when breaking out concrete floors and rock. Pneumatic drills back in the 1950s didn't have mufflers fitted to reduce noise levels and prolonged use caused deafness. Vibration also caused 'Carpal Tunnel Syndrome' that affected the wrist, upper arm and thumb. It was sometimes referred to as white finger. The dust generated by the use of pneumatic drills breaking out concrete floors and rock in confined places caused the disease 'Emphysema' that affected the lungs. Pneumatic drills were extensively used back in the 1950s before the introduction of hydraulic breakers.

Noise and dust were big problems when using rock drills. Many Irishmen were affected by at least one of the diseases mentioned above. Very few got compensation as they may have been working incognito, they were unable to prove the source of the disease and the company that employed them may have long since gone out of business. Many Irishmen suffered from more than one disease and for some it was rather tragic in that they wouldn't have family or friends to care for them. Some had to retire prematurely without any source of income, because they had worked under fictitious names, which resulted in hardship for their wives and family. Some returned to Ireland to their parents or a family member but the wife and children would remain in the UK. In some cases the parent's accommodation wouldn't be sufficient to cater for all the family so just the father would return. Benefits in the UK were more generous than in Ireland so the family stayed put. It was a sad situation that some families became fragmented in that way.

Bonus systems were always welcome but it was never very clear how certain things were measured to qualify for the different rates of pay. It was an incentive to work harder but it encouraged taking risks to qualify. Health and Safety wasn't as robust back in the 1950s and '60s. In many cases Irish men contracted skin diseases for not wearing protective clothing even when it was available. This applied particularly to men handling cement, diesel and other hazardous materials. Risks were less where men worked directly for companies but where work was contracted out, the risks became greater.

Mechanical excavators weren't widely used as they were too big and difficult to manoeuvre in restricted working areas. The big excavators at that time were Drag-line's and other big machines such as the Newton Chambers Koehring excavators (NCK's). They were a rather clumsy machine that had wire ropes for operating the back-actor equipment (the actual bucket). There were also the Ruston-Bucyrus cable excavators which back in the 1940s and '50s were known as 10 RB's and 22 RB's. Irishmen remained in big demand for groundwork such as drainage, big site excavations, work associated with kerb and slab laying and all kinds of concrete operations. Paddy with his shovel got the title of '*1 RB Paddy*'. Shovel power was in big demand for excavation work in housing estates and other large construction sites. The short handle shovel was a tool that took a bit of time to get used to especially for men arriving from Ireland for the first time. At home they were used to the long handle shovel but when they got used to using the short handle shovels they used to say, '*Sure 'tis easier to be a bit nearer the work than what it was in Ireland*' - meaning that they were further away from their work with the long handle shovels.

JCB's manufactured by JC Bamford and mini-excavators hadn't come to the fore in the construction and utilities industries. Some companies even went to Ireland to recruit men as they were regarded as being somewhat superior to their English counterparts where hand excavation work was concerned. Paddy was less likely to go on strike or become a trade union member.

Other big out of town contracts such as power stations, hydro electric work or dams in remote areas, particularly the north of Scotland, could present some problems for the company carrying out the work. Some of the main problems would be to recruit skilled labour and the transport required to take them to and from site daily. In most cases Irish labour was preferable for heavy excavation and concrete work. To help solve the daily transport problem of getting men to and from site, the company would provide a few big caravans on-site free of charge for some of their employees thus eliminating the travel problem. Public transport wouldn't be available or operate in most of these remote locations.

When contracts were complete, the caravans were moved to other remote sites. Of course it saved the company money long term in that they didn't have to pay travelling time and men could work late on into the evenings. Rates of pay for some of these big contracts were usually very attractive and the men got paid for a long weekend off-site every six weeks. Living conditions on-site could be a bit primitive but the big, strong Irishmen recruited for these contracts were prepared to sacrifice home comforts to maximise their earnings. The caravans would be a bit cramped with up to six men living in each one, but so long as they had beds, some cooking and washing facilities, they'd manage. However, bed clothes weren't washed and changed at regular intervals and the caravans weren't cleaned on a daily or even a weekly basis. The smell of smoke could be a bit overwhelming when everybody smoked in such confined areas. Of course, they could use some on-site facilities such as toilets. They wouldn't have any communication with home and it would be a time of concern for anybody that had left elderly parents behind. These caravans were hot in summertime and very cold in winter. I lived in one for a couple of months in Dumfries Scotland. A few of us rented it from a farmer just outside Dumfries. We were laying post office ducting for Alexander Thompson of Pipe Street, Portobello near Edinburgh. It was wintertime and it was frosty weather. The windows would have frost on the inside as there was no heating in it. It didn't have running water or a toilet but we didn't mind.

For those men on North of Scotland contracts, it would be a rather lonely six weeks period. Card playing or listening to the radio if one was available, were the only pass times. A company employee would be nominated to drive to the nearest shop and collect food, cigarettes or whatever else was required. When it came to the long weekends off-site the men would be taken to the nearest railway station possibly in a company mini bus. They'd return to London, Manchester, Glasgow or some other city or town and stay with friends, as they wouldn't have retained the accommodation that they previously lived in. The money saved over each six week period would be sent home to their parents or other family members. Sometimes the paper money would be crumpled and dirty having spent six weeks in the hip pockets of trousers. Dirty or crumpled, it was always welcome to the people back home in Ireland.

Life was rough and lonely working and living in these conditions far away from family and friends. Some of the big projects in the north of Scotland were Lough Awe and Lough Sloy. Almost all the men employed in these projects were from Mayo and Donegal. These men were good workers and always ready for a challenge even in rough conditions. Again they were to the fore in the construction of the Clyde Tunnel in Glasgow.

Having worked for a period of time with Wimpey or McAlpine's and other companies, many Irishmen became skilled in concrete work, kerbing and slab laying work and took advantage of these new skills. They'd take on private jobs in the evenings and at weekends such as foundations for extensions to houses, garages and walls. They'd lay slabs and concrete paths and also garage driveways. At that time mono-blocking was not a surface widely used if at all. Mono blocks are a bit like bricks in shape and size. Nowadays they are widely used for surfacing large areas in town centres, private properties, schools and hospitals as an alternative to concrete and tarmac surfaces. They can be purchased in various colours and laid in different configurations and greatly enhance the look of an area. Some companies would have a van for taking men to and from work and they'd use it for what they'd call their homers or private jobs. They might manage to get a few bags of cement or slabs for the smaller jobs from their place of employment by dropping the site foreman a few pounds in a matchbox. The matchbox was widely used as a means of passing money to a site foreman for any favours that he may have done for you.

For bigger jobs they'd get a supplier to deliver the materials direct to the job which could be building walls, a garage or a bit of drainage work. A bricklayer, joiner or other tradesman were hired where building house extensions or garages were involved. They too were always interested in a bit of extra cash. Sometimes it would be necessary to borrow a concrete mixer from their place of work for concreting jobs and mixing mortar, or a tipper lorry to remove surplus materials. It would be unlikely that they'd be involved in tipping charges as there was a lot of fly tipping in London at that time or for small amounts they'd tip it on the site where they worked.

For many it was a useful bit of extra income and helped to pay off mortgages or send money back to their family in Ireland. The smaller jobs were usually completed in a short time perhaps in a few evenings or a weekend. At that time it was cash in hand, so no tax deductions. Tax laws didn't appear to be as robust back in the 1950s as is currently the case. There was a lot of that kind of work available. It was a cost effective way for homeowners to get the work done, employing skilled labour rather than using a private company. The downside was that in the event of faulty workmanship it would be unlikely that the property owner would be successful in having remedial work carried out or obtain compensation. Generally, however, work was carried out to a satisfactory standard.

Another downside was that some self-employed men did a runner owing suppliers hundreds of pounds and in some cases many thousands. When pressure came from the supplier for payment they'd move to another area and change their name or perhaps move back to Ireland. This impacted on the authentic self-employed, so far as getting credit was concerned, even though they had always paid their dues. Perhaps I should make it clear that only a small number of self-employed would resort to doing a runner.

Many worked under assumed names and suppliers wouldn't have any hope of tracing them. When a job was finished and they were paid the agreed amount, greed took over on some occasions to the point that they couldn't even agree among themselves how the money should be divided. In some other cases, where materials were required to carry out the work such as sand, cement and bricks it would all be nicked from building sites. They'd have an arrangement with friends such as lorry drivers or foremen to nick materials for them and have them delivered to the site where the work was being carried out.

Likewise some Irish women made a bit of extra money in the evenings and at weekends doing a bit of casual hairdressing, baby sitting or even a spot of decorating and of course it would be cash in hand. They'd also take on house work for wealthy property owners. Some of the big property owners would have a number of houses or apartments that they'd rent out to various types of people such as business people, retired people, and factory and construction workers. The extra money for the girls would be a boost for those working in part time, poorly paid employment. Some could earn more money doing casual work and getting cash in hand than they could earn in their permanent full-time employment. They'd save it up for buying clothes or perhaps a holiday in Ireland or a bit of both as well as sending money home to help younger members of their families who were unemployed.

As I said earlier Irishmen and women were always willing and eager to avail of any opportunity that came their way to improve their lifestyle which was the main reason they left their homes in the first place.

At this point I think I should throw in this little story that I heard in London about some emigrants that went to London but one of them never wrote to his mother. That gentleman was called Dunne, and not only didn't he write home but he never went home. Some of his neighbouring friends went home on holiday so when they visited his mother. She asked, '*Do you ever see my son over there?*' Charlie said, '*I see him occasionally but I don't have his address.*' "*When you go back to London if you see him ask him why the hell he doesn't write home"*. She then said, '*I'm not sure of his address but I think it finishes up with WC1.*' Charlie wasn't the brightest but one day he was down the West End and he saw a WC so he thought to himself that must be where your man lives. He went downstairs and knocked on one of the doors. A man from inside answered, '*Yes.*' Then Charlie asked, '*Are you Dunne*' and the man answered, '*Yes.*' Charlie then said, "*Well why the hell don't you write home to your mother*".

James Quinlivan 1910
my father b.1890

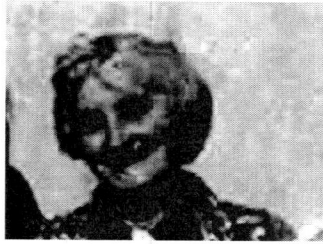

Mary Reid Quinlivan,
Mother, b.1895

Joe Quinlivan 1956

2012
I visit my father's old home now deserted

L-R my sister Mary,
daughter Teresa
Mary and my
mother 1966

Old School Lisseycasey 1948 Headmaster Seamus Kellerher, I am back row extreme right

Corncrake

Bringing in the turf, ploughing and haymaking   © Clare Library

Ennis 1950

CIE bus Leyland
Tiger PS 2 Model
fleet number P347
©Michael Corcoran
National Transport
Museum

O'Connell Street,
Limerick.

Dublin 1950

Holyhead Old Hotel and Train at the Station

Princess Maude

Blarney Club

Sacred Heart Quex Road Kilburn

M. J. Clancy 1950s
1st office
Wembley High Road London
© Clancy Group

M. J.Clancy
acquired old
concrete works
Harefield
Middlesex
© Clancy Group

M. J. Clancy new offices
MJC in suit left
© Clancy Group

L-R Gerry Armory,
Tom Gohery, Keith
Oswald,
Con O'Brien senior
positions Clancy
Group–now retired
© Clancy Group

*McNicholas
Construction
cable laying
operation
1950s
© McNicholas*

*Murphy's 1960
typical early
utilities project
© Murphy
Group*

*Murphy's 1960
Post Office installation, The Mall,
London. © Murphy Group*

*Murphy's 1950s dredged
aggregates docking facility
© Murphy Group*

Murphy's 1950s sea dredged aggregates docking facility © Murphy Group

Murphys 1960s gas pipeline for North Western Gasboard © Murphy Group

ClancyDocwra a trencher excavating on carriageway conveyor belt loading © Clancy Group

Murphy's 1960 Construction of a cable tunnel in Birmingham © Murphy Group

Murphy wagons 1960 plant yard London © Murphy Group

Rowton House,
Camden Town
© Peter Higginbotham

Petticoat Lane
© Bishopgate Ins.
D31(36)

Speaker's corner
1950s
© Bob Collins
Image

Galtymore

Malachy Sweeney © Reynolds family

Best man at my friend's wedding Joe Quinlivian (no relation) in London in the late 1950s. I am standing next to the groom.

Harlesden trolleybus

The Crown Pub, Cricklewood

The Spotted Dog. Willesdon

Gleeson construction site in Chesterfield © M.J.Gleeson

Joe & Bridgetta in Trafalgar Square 1960

Wedding Day May 5th 1962 in Falkirk

Going to a wedding 1996

In California 2002

Joe and Bridgetta's 50th Wedding Anniversary 2012
Back Row L-R: Anthony, Annmarie, Claire, Frances
Front Row L-R: Pauline, Bridgetta, Teresa Mary, Joe
and remembering James (deceased)

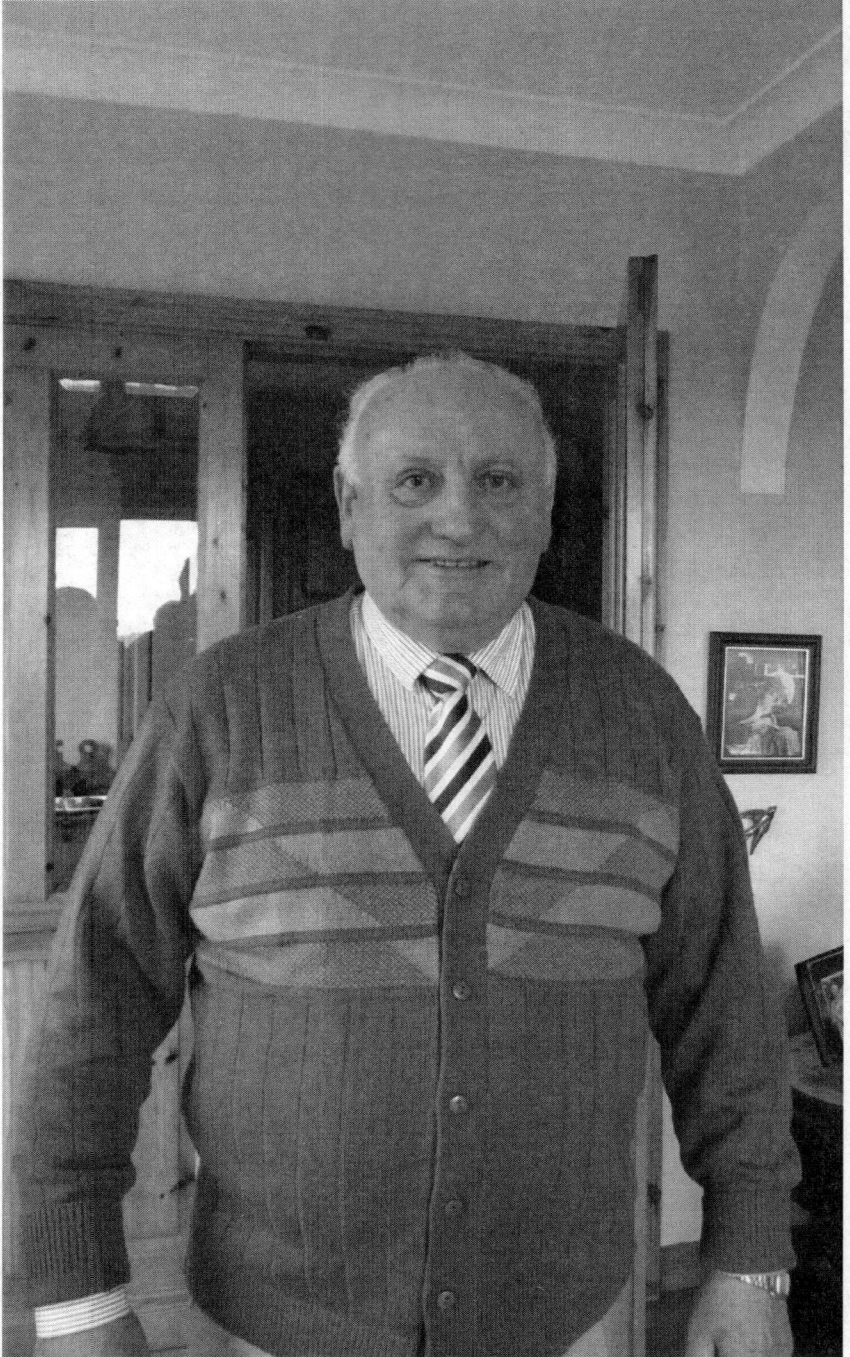

Joe Quinlivan, 2014

15.
Dangerous Working Conditions

Working with cement, whether wet or dry, without the proper hand and body protection could be hazardous and many suffered from a skin inflammation called dermatitis. Another health hazard was working with asbestos in confined places like tunnels. Asbestos rope or string was used for sealing the joints of the tunnel rings to prevent water seepage and of course tunnels were confined places. The dangerous part of the operation was sealing the joints above one's head when asbestos fibres were dropping down and being inhaled. A very dear friend of mine who worked in tunnels got that deadly disease called asbestosis. Back in the 1950s and '60s the proper protective clothing wasn't supplied for working with such a hazardous material, but at that time health authorities weren't aware of the risks. Asbestos rope sealing was widely used in the construction of the Clyde Tunnel and indeed many others.

I recall working in High Wycombe outside London where we were sinking a pumping station for a sewerage system and the excavation was pile driven. It had a high water table so it was necessary to seal the pile joints to prevent water entering the excavation. Asbestos rope was used and one of our colleagues who was assigned to doing that job suffered from asbestosis some twenty years later and died. Sadly his wife couldn't claim compensation as the contractor that employed him wasn't paying a block insurance.

I got a job with a sub-contractor labouring in the construction industry working five and a half days a week @ £2.10 shillings per day from Monday to Friday and £4 for a half day on Saturday, making a total of £16.10 shillings per week. As they'd say in London the work was dog rough. However, £16.10 shillings was considered a good wage in 1955 /56. On some occasions we'd have to work all day in the rain, sometimes without a break. There were no drying facilities to dry clothes overnight. Often wet to the skin one had to endure travelling for over an hour in the back of a van to get back to Harlesden. Yes, the money was hard earned but nevertheless one appreciated being in employment. The sites that I worked in were mostly in Bushey and Wheathampstead. It was dangerous working uninsured and many Irishmen were involved in accidents which meant they had to pay for treatment and in the case of serious injury they couldn't seek compensation. Not many Irishmen working incognito for sub-contractors had a bank account or a post office savings account for obvious reasons. Some would save up as much money as possible for a few weeks and then put it into an envelope and send it home to Ireland. Some of it would be destined for their parents and the rest for the Bank of Ireland. For parents opening an envelope that contained a number of nice crisp white Bank of England £5 notes, it was like winning the lottery. The English £5 note was a big white note with the Bank of England written on it.

It was rough and sometimes dangerous work particularly laying deep pipe work for drainage as from time to time men were injured when there was a ground collapse due to inadequate shuttering (planks of wood or sheet piles to support the sides of excavations).

I recall a job installing a large 24 or 30 inch sewer pipe in a deep trench on the outskirts of Wheathampstead when the sides of the trench collapsed. It was up to 10 feet in depth. Two of my work colleagues were trapped and it took a bit of frantic digging to get them out. Luckily they weren't seriously hurt but hurt nonetheless and both were badly shocked. They were working together near the mouth of the last pipe that they had installed when the ground collapsed. They managed to crawl into the pipe, which saved them from the second collapse which was pretty substantial. The pipe was open at both ends so they had plenty of air and oxygen. They could have crawled through the pipe and got out at the other end but they were too shocked. However, nobody was aware that they had managed to crawl inside the pipe 'till all the collapsed soil was excavated down to the mouth of it. The trench had shuttering at intervals but it was totally inadequate for the ground conditions and the depth of the excavation. A contributing factor to the second and more substantial ground collapse was a fractured water main nearby. The ganger took the injured and shocked men to the site cabin and got them a cup of tea. One was complaining about a pain in his shoulder and the other had some heavy bruising in his back but neither got any medical attention. They stayed on site for the rest of the day 'till finishing time. It was necessary for both men to have some time off work to recuperate but they didn't get paid as they were working incognito and on a shift - work basis.

In most cases at that time ladders weren't provided for men entering and exiting deep excavations. Men usually climbed in and out by using the struts which were cross pieces of the shuttering as ladders. When one stepped on to the top strut it sometimes collapsed with the weight and then when the person fell on to the strut below it too may collapse. On many occasions men sustained serious injury. Knocking out a section of the ground support could then trigger a ground collapse and a person or persons could be buried. This is something I saw happen on a number of occasions. Some contractors weren't concerned about men working in a safe environment; getting the job done as quickly as possible regardless of hazards was the objective. Gangers in most cases got a bonus to get the job finished in the shortest possible time.

At that time all site facilities were a bit primitive in that water for washing hands was usually a big pail or similar which everybody used. At one of the Bushey sites we had a tea boy, whom I'll call Bert, but that wasn't his real name. He wasn't too keen on some of the Irish lads on site, one or two in particular. One day he decided to put laxatives in some cups of tea for the Irish boys and, yes, it had the desired affect. A Tipperary lad called Christy Delaney who was one of the recipients that suffered the affects of the laxatives thought of an idea to return Bert the compliment. Away in the corner of the field there was a little toilet cubicle. It had a big tub-like, half barrel container with a board across the top as a seat and the container was almost full. Of course it was intended to reach that stage for the maximum effect. Christy told everyone in the Irish squad and a few others of his intended plan to pay back Bert. He cut the board from the underside up leaving just a small margin to keep it intact. Bert went inside closed the door and took a seat. It went down with a bang so it was a repetition of what happened to "Old King Cole". He emerged in a bit of a state heavily stained with some of the laxative product in evidence around the nether region and shall we say not smelling of roses. He was furious saying, *'I'd like to know who the b......d was that cut the toilet seat.'* When the dust settled, not that there was a lot of it, one of the boys got some water, helped to clean him up and gave him an old pair of trousers. Later on that day, Christy told him that it was he who cut the seat to get his own back. They both shook hands and called it quits. Bert's own countrymen were not very keen on him either as allegedly he was stealing money from their jackets and trousers which were hanging in the cabin which was used for changing their clothes.

Other labouring jobs on-site were offloading bricks and cement. At that time bags of cement were one hundred and twelve pounds or one hundred weight and still very hot when they arrived on site. The bricks were usually delivered from Leighton Buzzard brickworks. Gloves were not provided for handling the bricks or cement so everybody had sore, raw finger tops.

Travel to and from a site in Bushey was one hour plus each way in the back of a van driven by a John McCall. It would be about 7.30 pm when we arrived back at Nichol Road, Harlesden, which was the dropping off point so it was a bit of a rush to get some grub before the shops closed. Thomas was our local butcher and Lambert's our local greengrocer. Mr Lambert told me a funny story about an Irishman that frequented his shop. One day the Irishman entered the shop and was eyeing up the Brussels sprouts and thought they were small cabbages. After a while he said to Mr Lambert, *'your cabbages are very small in this man's country sure I'll need at least a dozen of them.'* Mr Lambert explained that they weren't cabbages, but the Irishman wasn't convinced.

I recall working on a job at Gloucester Road, London in the late 1950s. It was near the West London Air Terminal and the job was installing an eighteen way post office ducting. The contractor was John Murphy & Sons Ltd. and a Mr Foley from Kerry was the ganger man. A lot of Kerry men were working on that job and some were very good workers. It was necessary to revert to short headings at interchange sections and traffic lights. They had to excavate test holes along the intended route to check for other buried plant such as water and gas mains. The Londoners or Cockneys going to work couldn't understand the idea of excavating holes and backfilling them again. They were very polite people and as they passed by an excavation they'd tilt their bowler hat and say, '*Mornin Pat have you found it yet.*' as though Paddy was looking for something he'd lost or was digging for oil. With the sun beaming down on a shirtless Paddy and the skin peeling off his back and not a lot of oxygen in an excavation site at some five or six feet below the surface he'd say, '*Ah sure Jaysus I think I'll have to go a bit deeper yet.*' As our English friends went on their way they'd say, '*Have a nice day at the office Pat.*'

At that time mostly all Cockneys carried a brief case as a kind of status symbol. Bowler hat and brief case were rather alien to Paddy whose status symbol was a white handkerchief knotted at the four corners, a foot iron and Yorks. A lot of our English friends would only have two slices of bread with drip and the Daily Mail in the brief case. Some would have one with and one without drip as the one without was a half pence cheaper than the one with. Paddy might say, '*Have you got your two slices of drip this morning. Jaysus you wouldn't dig much on two slices of drip.*'

Our English friends couldn't understand the mentality of us Irish and likewise we couldn't understand theirs. The one difference, however, was that most of our English friends were educated and we were not. When they climbed the ladder in their place of employment it meant promotion but when poor Paddy climbed the ladder it meant that he was either a hod carrier or he was going into or coming out of a deep excavation.

16.
Working on Gas Contracts

During the late 1950s I worked on many gas contracts around London, Scotland and Wales. One of the first jobs on gas was in South East London and I think it was late 1957 or 58. It was repair work on an eighteen inch medium pressure main with working pressure of 5PSI or five pounds per square inch of pipe. Some medium pressure mains operated at much higher pressures. It was the old town gas and it was very toxic with carbon monoxide. The company carrying out the work was William Press and Son Limited of Willoughey Lane, Tottenham, London. Their slogan was *'Complete Service to Industry'*. They were carrying out the work on behalf North Thames Gas. They sub-let the excavation work to a sub-contractor. I am not sure if it was Chambers, Kennedy or De Lacy. There were about a dozen men split into teams of two or three. We were paid £5 per shift Monday to Friday, £7.10 shillings for all day Saturday and £10 for Sunday or a total of £42.10 shillings for the seven shifts. It was very good money at that time, but the reason that the shift rate was so generous was the fact that it was difficult to retain the necessary numbers of men, due the heavy digging, and to the hazardous working conditions.

The main was laid at a depth of about four feet to the top. It was on a carriageway and it was extremely dangerous work. Some of the old joints were passing a lot of gas and some big deposits had built up under the surface of the carriageway. There were different types of joints such as Stanton Wilson, hook bolts and t-bolts. Some of the bolts were either missing or broken.

We were issued with spark proof tools such as shovels and picks, but when rock and stone deposits built up on the tools they were no longer spark proof. There were a number of explosions where heavy gas deposits had built up and some men sustained burns to their hands, face and hair. We were issued with gas masks but they were only worn when we got below the surface level. We had some characters among the team such as Spider Murphy, Toothache O'Hara and Woodbine Casey. Spider was a real character with some great sayings. When the going got a bit rough he'd say, *'Jaysus a man would be as well off dead in America.'* When somebody was telling him a story with too many ifs he'd say, *'Jaysus 'tis if if if, if, my auntie had b...'s sure she'd be my uncle.'* Then out of the blue he'd say, *'She won't be long gone soon.'* He was 'real cool' as they'd say in America. He didn't like wearing a gas mask and he'd get gassed a few times a day. I think he was from the Castleisland area of County Kerry but at that time Spider could have been from anywhere.

The masks weren't cleaned properly and some men pulled them down below their nose but kept the mouth covered. They didn't realise that they were inhaling gas through the nose. It was difficult working with a mask on as the face-piece would steam up and impair one's vision. It was unhygienic passing masks one to another particularly where men had rashes and boils. The masks would become smelly and sweaty. It was an inexpensive way of getting drunk but anybody that got gassed then suffered from a very severe headache. Some drank fizzy lemonade in an effort to purge the gas out of their system. I was gassed on a few occasions but as soon as I felt I was getting light headed I'd leave the excavation and surrounding area immediately. I recall the very severe headaches that ensued. It was only possible to work for short periods when excavating and cleaning the hard, dry, powder like substance from around the joints. When a man passed out down at the bottom of an excavation it would be difficult to get him to the surface and sometimes the men that were carrying out the rescue were also overcome. On some occasions it would be necessary to call an ambulance twice or even three times to site on the same day. Some men were taken to hospital in an unconscious state and I saw men being stretchered away in an ambulance still wearing their Irish safety helmet (*white handkerchief*) and sometimes only wearing their trousers. Some men were detained in hospital overnight and for many it could be embarrassing in that they wouldn't have any underwear.

The joint repairs were carried out by the company's own men but their output may only be a few joints per day. They were qualified to work on live gas operations and had the correct safety clothing and equipment. They had a big cabin on-site where they spent most of the day reading newspapers and having a kip / sleep from time to time.

The contract was for two months duration and we mostly worked seven days per week. The good thing was that we were paid properly every week, unlike some other gas contracts that I worked on.

Many men lived in rented accommodation, some lived in full board and a few were sleeping rough. Large concrete pipes, from memory they were thirty or thirty six inch diameter pipes, were stacked nearby associated with a drainage/sewerage contract, and they were the accommodation for the few men sleeping rough. These men managed to get one of the on-site drivers to take them to a farm to get some straw. They stuffed one end of the pipe which they occupied with straw to stop the draught and then used some more of it to lie on. It was a bit like a block of flats without a front, in that men slept at different levels. It was a rough way to live as they wouldn't have a proper wash or change of clothes from Monday to Friday. At the weekends they'd stay with a friend in London and get a proper wash and a change of clothes and that was it for another week.

During the week they went straight to the pub in the evenings and then got a bit of grub in a café before settling down for the night in their respective concrete pipes. The weather was warm and the concrete pipes retained a lot of heat well into the night. Their night attire was wearing the same clothes that they had worn at work during the day. On one occasion local residents called the police as their new neighbours arrived back from the pub heavily intoxicated late at night.

Initially they kept the place tidy but after a couple of weeks there was a lot of debris thrown about the place such as milk bottles, empty cigarette packets, bits of bread and old newspapers. Some mornings one or two of them would arrive on site straight out of their concrete pipe unwashed and in an intoxicated state from the night before. They wouldn't have any money to buy breakfast and they'd be in a foul mood. They'd be looking for money or a sub off the other men but without success in most cases. They'd then nick sandwiches from the William Press men, be abusive, cursing and swearing and not in any fit state to work.

Sometimes when an excavation was water logged, they'd wear old discarded wellington boots that were the property of the William Press team. The boots would be piled outside the cabin sometimes wet on the inside and if they couldn't find a matching pair they would wear two right or two left boots.

The rest of the Irish lads would be disgusted at their behaviour and make their feelings known to them. The contractor carrying out the drainage work evicted them saying, '*Animals wouldn't live in the conditions that they lived.*' They then moved into an old derelict building and then a short while later they were put off site by the William Press foreman as his own men were complaining about them. It was much too dangerous to have intoxicated men working in an area with a heavy gas presence. It was a minority of men who lived like that, moving about from company to company, that gave the Irish a bad name.

You really would not know the names of any of these men because at that time they operated under fictitious names. It was often the case that a working colleague on a particular job known as Murphy may well be Casey the next time that one met him. And some time later the same gentleman may be Flanagan or O'Reilly so it was almost impossible for the Revenue to keep track of him. Of course that was the idea to get 'baptised' at regular intervals and change the name.

The next gas contract was in Long Parish in Hampshire. Again William Press & Son Ltd. secured the contract to install a mile of twelve inch diameter cast iron main along a carriageway. The pipe jointing, testing and commissioning was carried out by the company's own men. They sub- let the excavation and backfill work to sub-contractors. However, I think I should make it clear that regardless which contractor it was they were reputable sub-contractors but some of the men that they employed as agents and quantity surveyors were sharks. In most cases the contractor wouldn't be aware of the dodges that some of their agents got up to such as on day-work jobs (paid by the shift so called) they'd book in '*dead men*' - men that didn't exist. They usually collected the wages in brown packets or lump sums from the contractor's office and pocketed the dead men's wages. They fiddled their own countrymen out of hard earned money.

There were eight men in the team and we were paid per linear yard. We had to lower the pipes manually into the excavation and thread them along the bottom under existing services. For that we were paid a day-work rate which only amounted to a few hours per week for assisting with the pipe laying. The William Press men were friendly but gave Paddy a wide berth and I suppose in some cases with good reason. They weren't too keen on any heavy lifting or getting their hands dirty but they allowed us to use their onsite facilities for making tea or having a bit of a fry up. We got £1.12.6 per linear yard to excavate and backfill. The pipes were eighteen feet in length or six linear yards. The minimum cover on carriageways was two feet and six inches but due to existing services it was necessary to lay the pipes much deeper at various intervals. The joints were lead run and extra width was required for caulking up the joints. Mick Cassins a Dublin man, was the pipe jointer and a specialist on lead joints. He was always good to share a joke with and a gentleman. The extra width and depth was paid per cubic yard but the extra road base depth was where we were fiddled by our own countrymen, as I'll explain later. At that time almost every agreement was by word of mouth and very rarely would Irish navvies get anything in writing.

The big compressor was either a Broomwade or Ingersoll Rand, but I think it was a Broomwade on iron wheels. It was heavy to move about and it operated four pneumatic breakers or jack hammers. The breakers were heavy and clumsy and I think they were McDonalds. In cold weather conditions it took six men to start the compressor. It was necessary to put a rope on the handle so it was one man on the handle and two men on either side pulling the rope. One man operated the levers. There were six in number and they were put in a vertical position until the men operating the handle shouted at the man on the levers 'Pull them down.' This process may have to be repeated a number of times before the compressor burst into life.

Technology to locate underground plant such as water mains and cables wasn't available, resulting in a lot of damage. One man damaged an electric cable and his right arm was badly burned. He was taken to hospital and I believe he returned to Ireland after his discharge. Damage to a water main or service resulted in the excavation being flooded and that meant lost production time. We sometimes worked in the rain to make a decent week's wage. Clothes would be dirty and wet working down in a deep excavation and nowhere to dry them overnight except inside the compressor room. It retained a lot of heat when the side flaps were closed at the end of the day's work.

It was rumoured some subcontractor's agents and quantity surveyors were on the fiddle when it came to measuring the extra width and depth and also the extra road base and day-work hours. The Quantity Surveyor would be getting a brown envelope to enhance the cubic measurements. Then there would be arguments every Friday (measure day) with the Agent about being short measured. The problem was that none of the workers could calculate the various cubic measurements but were fully aware that they were being short measured. These were the preferred type of men, the thicker the better for the contractor's Agent and the Quantity Surveyor.

Our William Press foreman was a Londoner called Jack Stockbridge. He had a little van and I travelled with him back to London any weekend that we weren't working. He smoked a pipe and always had a dog with him in the van. He was a gentleman. Four weeks into the contract I asked Jack could it be possible that we were being short changed. He said that he would take the matter up with his Director and he was true to his word. He called a meeting with the sub-contractor and the result was that their payments were put on hold until it was established if in fact we were being short measured and by how much. The contractor was requested to excavate test holes, at their expense, at intervals along the completed section to establish the correct cubic measurements for the various categories. Should it be the case that the measurements were proved to be correct they would be paid for the excavation of the test holes. The Director made it clear that he wouldn't get involved with the rates we were being paid by the contractor. The end result was that we got in excess of £80 per man back pay and an apology from the contractor.

Soon after the contract started a couple of men left and day-work hours continued to be claimed for them. The contractor would probably think that it was all above board but somebody, other than the agent, should have been aware that men were being fiddled. On the other hand, the agent put an amount through each week, went to the office and collected a lump sum and then stuffed a brown envelope for each man on-site.

The quantity surveyor worked independently of Jack Stockbridge. He, like the contractor's agent was responsible for a number of sites and only visited our site on a Friday. The agent and the quantity surveyor were dismissed or perhaps it was an Alan Sugar *'you're fired'*. Also the contractor had to reimburse William Press for the overcharges and fraudulent measurement claims but there was a compromise on the reimbursement of the overcharge for the day-work hours. Only for the fact that their own quantity surveyor authenticated the measurements for the day-work hours claimed and the fact that they were unable to establish who initiated the scam the contractor would have been thrown off site.

As I mentioned earlier dodges and scams like the one I've highlighted above   sometimes weighted heavily against a contractor tendering for work, regardless how competitive he might be.   However, the incentive to fiddle may be that a company foreman or quantity surveyor may be on a rather low wage and the contractor's agent on a bonus system. Bonus for the agent would be based on net weekly values so any additional revenue generated contributed towards that as well as the unclaimed brown envelopes for the dead men. Greed then takes over.

Thereafter we were paid the correct measurements thanks to Jack Stockbridge and his Director. It may have been the case that the contractor was not aware of the on-site rackets since the agent was responsible for a few more sites. The contractor had a lot of contracts in the South of England and blamed his accountant for not bringing it to his attention but, at that time, these rackets were pretty widespread and common among mostly all sub-contractors.

Jack Stockbridge appreciated the work that we were doing in difficult circumstances. When the main-laying was finished and the main was commissioned after approximately three months work, the contractor didn't get any more work on-site. There were services to be transferred from the old main to the new one and we were asked by Jack Stockbridge if we'd do the excavation and reinstatement work on a day-work basis. We all stayed on and were paid £6 per shift net. William Press took care of our tax and insurance deductions, although we didn't get a pay-slip. That gave us another six week's work. William Press were a good company to work for and one got paid whatever the agreed figure was, either verbally or in writing, but as I stated earlier mostly all agreements were verbal.

Many Irishmen were fiddled by their own countrymen but it wasn't confined to just sub-contractors. Many bar staff and landladies were effectively dipping their hand into their countrymen's pockets.

17.
Some Big Contracts outside London

During the 1950s and 1960s there were some big construction sites outside London such as Fawley and the Isle of Grain. The Isle of Grain was a very large oil refinery constructed during the 1950s and the early part of the 1960s. I believe it was operated by British Petroleum. It employed thousands of Irishmen and some of the big companies that employed them were MacAlpine, Wimpey and Costain-John Brown. Some were directly employed by the companies but many were employed by sub-contractors. It was convenient enough for London and for the large numbers of Irishmen living in Camden Town, Kilburn and Cricklewood and elsewhere in London. I worked there in 1956 but I only stayed a few weeks.

Site accommodation was rough and the camps were overcrowded and in some cases not very hygienic. Food and drink were available on site. It was difficult to get to sleep at night as some men would be drunk and creating a disturbance. However, some men travelled daily to and from site in a fleet of buses. The men that lived on-site would go to London at weekends. Noise and dust were pretty severe on site during the day and many men were injured. It was a massive site but isolated, and could be a place in the Nevada Desert, although it was only thirty to forty miles from London. Fawley Oil Refinery near Southampton also employed large numbers of Irishmen in the early 1950s. It too was a massive site but didn't have as many sub-contractors as the Isle of Grain. Other big projects at that time were Motorways, the London Underground, British Railways and Tunnel work such as the Clyde, Mersey and Dartford.

Following is a little song that some of the lads on the Isle of Grain job used to sing and it was called McAlpine's Fusiliers.

McAlpine's Fusiliers
As down the Glen came McAlpine's men
With their shovels slung behind them
'Twas in the pub they drank the sub
And up in the Spike you'll find them.

They sweated blood and washed down mud
With pints and quarts of beer
And now we're on the road again
With McAlpine's Fusiliers.

I stripped to the skin with the Darky Finn
Way down in the Isle of Grain
With the Horse-face Toole I knew the rule
No money if you stop for rain.

McAlpine's God was a well filled hod
Your shoulders cut to bits and seared
And woe to the man who looks for tea
With McAlpine's Fusiliers.

These men were made of steel
They just didn't have any fears
Oh these were the days when men were men
The McAlpine Fusiliers.

There was dragline O'Hara and bulldog McGhee
Who ate some boiled ham raw
They'd sleep under a bush or maybe a hedge
Or a field on a bale of straw.

I remember the day that the Bear O'Shea
Fell into a concrete stairs
What the Horse-face said when he saw him dead
Well it wasn't what one would call prayers.

I'm a navvy short was his one retort
That reached unto my ears
When the going is rough you must be tough
With McAlpine's Fusiliers.

I've worked 'till the sweat it has me bet
With Russian, Czeck and Pole
On shuddering jams up in the hydro dams
Or underneath the Thames in a hole.

I grafted hard and I got me cards
And many a ganger's fist across me ears
If you pride yourself don't join by Christ
McAlpine's Fusiliers.

18.
Accommodation

One of my first addresses in January 1955 was in Ruckledge Avenue, Harlesden, London, N.W.10. The rent was fifteen shillings or £1 each per week which was the going rate at that time. I was sharing a second floor apartment with five other men. Sharing accommodation was a means of keeping costs to a minimum. Full occupation of an apartment meant the landlord could be competitive with the weekly rent. The Ruckledge Avenue accommodation was a bit overcrowded in that six people were sharing a rather small apartment. Five were Clare men and one a Limerick man. It was clean and had a friendly atmosphere. However, it had only one toilet which was shared by everyone and no bathroom.

It was better than other accommodation that I experienced later in Bathurst Gardens near Kensal Green. The rooms were small as they had been sub divided from larger rooms. They were called bed sits which was rather appropriate in that one had to literally sit on the single bed and keep one's case under it. The rooms or cubicles weren't much larger than the size of some of today's big built in wardrobes. Some didn't even have a window and were more like a prison cell. The rent was twelve shillings and six pence per week. Most rooms had a small single wardrobe and a small locker at the side of the bed. There was a narrow passage with rooms on either side. At the top of the stairs there was a gas cooker to be shared by all on that floor. A shilling meter was in a cupboard above it but the problem was when the gas went out 'twas the same people who ended up putting the shilling in it all the time. Men smoked indoors at that time. It was also unhygienic cooking meals in the landing with the smell of smoke from the cooker.

When one cooked a bit of grub it was necessary to take it to the room, place the plate on top of the locker and sit on the bed. The landing also had a big old smelly refrigerator for everybody to store their perishables. It was totally inadequate to store food for at least six people. It was never defrosted or cleaned. Food such as rotted chicken and pieces of uncooked bacon had maggots proving that the temperature setting was too low or perhaps non-existent. This I witnessed with my own eyes. I kept what I could in the little locker but confined the purchasing of food to small amounts on a daily basis to ensure freshness. Another problem with the refrigerator was people stealing food from their colleague tenants, particularly when fresh food was deposited. Milk was about four pence a pint, a loaf of bread about four to five pence and a dozen eggs about twelve or fifteen pence. Best frying steak was half a crown to three shillings a pound. The currency at that time was the old pound, shillings and pence.

It was pretty noisy with men coming and going particularly at weekends. The problem with that type of rented accommodation was that one never knew what type of character one was sharing with. A couple of the cubicles were in a filthy state and weren't fit for cattle. The characters that lived in them were dirty and one had boils in the back of his neck as big as plums. It was unhygienic to share accommodation with people like that although some spoke to the landlord expressing their concerns about the situation but he wasn't prepared to do anything about it. The landlord lived elsewhere in London and had absolutely no concern about the welfare of his tenants. Unfortunately and I'm sad to say it, but he was Irish. For him it was simply a case of getting the maximum rent value out of the property. The bed sits could be lonely places in the absence of television or somebody to talk to. I only stayed there for a few months and moved to another address in Bathurst Gardens with a bit more room space and better regulated in that the landlord and landlady were living on the premises.

Some men lived in hostels sometimes referred to as '*Rowton houses*' or '*dosshouses*'. Camden Town, Elephant and Castle and Hammersmith used to have these places. They were mostly built at the end of the 19th century for single men by the philanthropist Lord Rowton. They were rough places but at least people had a roof over their head.

Most men living in rented accommodation wouldn't have time to make breakfast from Monday to Friday. They wouldn't have time to wash their hair or brush their teeth and some didn't have any to brush. It was a tough life particularly in winter, travelling long journeys in the backs of wagons without any heat. Many travelled considerable distances out of London to work each morning and it would be a bit of a rush to catch a Murphy, McNicholas or Lowry wagon or van. If they missed their transport it would mean a lost shift as public transport wouldn't be available for most journeys or if it was available it would take too long to get there. Breakfast would be at a café later in the morning adjacent to where the job was. Sometimes it would be a midday breakfast and evening meal all rolled into one.

At the weekend it would be a big cooked breakfast in their rented accommodation. Again it would be the full works such as steak, sausages, mushrooms, black pudding and eggs. I often thought it was a miracle that people didn't suffer from food poisoning. Cooking utensils weren't kept clean. Like some old cars the big frying pan would be long overdue a change of oil and decoke.

Cooking was a skill most Irishmen didn't have when they left Ireland but many soon picked up basic cooking such as frying, boiling a bit of meat, vegetables and spuds, but it wouldn't be to the Jamie Oliver standard. However, there were some that weren't too fussy about washing up the utensils and cleaning up their accommodation in general. The cooker, floor and surrounding areas on occasions would be well greased with splashes of cooking oil out of the frying pan. Some who may have a sister living nearby or a girlfriend would come along at intervals and do the necessary but very soon it would be back to how it was originally.

Gas cookers were dangerous for some men returning at night who might be rather intoxicated. They would put potatoes or vegetables on to boil and then return to their room and fall asleep. When the pot boiled over it extinguished the flame. The smell of the old town gas would be throughout the upstairs area.

When I worked in the Port Talbot area of South Wales it was difficult to find suitable accommodation to rent, so it had to be full board and lodging. The food would be ideal for somebody on a slimming programme. Breakfast was a poached egg and beans, tea, bread and butter. I said tea, bread and butter but the butter was margarine. The landlady used to put margarine into a butter paper to give the impression that it was butter as no doubt she thought that Paddy wouldn't know the difference.

One day big Christy a Cork man said to her, *'I hope Mrs you didn't get charged for butter when you bought that lot, that's bloody margarine.'* She was really embarrassed and denied it was margarine. She said, *'I'll take it back to the shop where I bought it and ask to have it checked.'* Of course she didn't do that but we got what looked more like butter thereafter, but some of the boys weren't convinced and suspected that it was a mixture of butter and margarine. Dinner was mostly fish and chips with plenty peas. On some occasions we'd get a thin slice of beef floating on gravy with lashings of peas and a couple of boiled potatoes. The gravy would be running over the edge of the plate and Tommy a Mayo man said to the landlady one evening, *'Jaysus Mrs we'll need a two inch pump to keep the gravy out, the plates are flooded.'* She commented, *'Some of you Irishmen are never happy.'*

One of the men had false teeth and at meal times he used to rattle them around in his mouth to annoy another lodger; Tommy Brennan or Brannon. He used to leave his teeth on a small table at his bedside. One night Tommy went into his room and swapped the teeth for another set that were much bigger. That stopped the teeth clattering in that they didn't fit. It would be some time before he managed to get another set.

Perhaps I should say here that some landladies didn't understand that most Irishmen had ferocious appetites and couldn't survive on the type of food they were being given. It would be fair to say that most landladies did make the effort to accommodate Irishmen's appetites but there were the devious one's also.

Some of the rooms and beds were rarely cleaned and some beds had fleas. Tommy Brennan/ Brannon said to the landlady one morning, *'Do you know Mrs I've nearly lost a stone in weight over the past couple of weeks.'* She asked, *'Are you dieting.'* He said, *'No Mrs, dieting is not necessary in here between the bad grub and being eaten with fleas sure Jaysus you'd soon lose weight.'* There were often two men to a bed, which was perhaps to ensure that the fleas were well fed. The Landlady was rather greedy in that she endeavoured to squeeze in as many men as possible. Accommodation at that time was a bit difficult to find and she felt confident that she would always find enough people. There was only one toilet for seven men so some mornings they'd be a queue, especially if one or two were on the beer the night before. The toilet paper was old newspapers cut into squares on a wire hook. It only had a wash hand basin and no bath. There was a notice on the outside of the toilet door saying 'When this toilet is busy or there is an emergency please use the overflow toilet at the bottom of the backyard.' There was a dry toilet in the backyard, but it didn't have the luxury toilet paper that was in the inside toilet so one may have to resort to the freshly grown toilet paper - the grass! It didn't have a door but it was facing a high wall so it wasn't a place to read a newspaper or fall asleep. Not many were brave enough to use it with the exception of flies. One wouldn't be safe using it if one didn't have a mask and protective clothing. Overflow was very appropriate. It was easily the worst accommodation that I was ever in, but it wasn't easy to find an alternative.

Four of us moved to other accommodation after a couple of weeks and I think it was to York Place. The rooms were clean and comfortable and the food was better and it was flea free. There was a bathroom, a separate toilet and plenty of good toilet paper. However, the rooms were pretty cold as it was winter and they didn't have central heating. Some rooms had paraffin heaters, but they were a bit smelly and weren't sufficient to heat a big room, but it was like the Dorchester Hotel in comparison to the previous accommodation. The other three lads moved out from the previous accommodation a couple of weeks later and allegedly the morning that they were leaving one of them, a Tony Sweeney either a Leitrim or Roscommon man, stuck a Kipper to the bottom of the table. Tony said, *'That'll put a bit of a smell about the place after a couple of days and it will be rather difficult to find.'*

Most accommodation associated with apartment or room letting didn't have either a bath or shower so a bath was a once a week occasion and a bit of a treat. Of course most people from rural Ireland weren't accustomed to having a bath before they left home as running water and electricity was non existent. Most Irishmen working in construction didn't have a bath at home in Ireland. It would only be in summer in very warm weather conditions that people would go and have a wash in a secluded spot at perhaps a cascade or a little waterfall. I think people only washed their face hands and feet most of the year and occasionally washed their hair.

In London most Irishmen living in rented accommodation such as bedsits depended on the public baths for a weekly wash. So for Irishmen living in the Harlesden or Kensal Green areas it was down the Harrow Road on a Sunday morning to the public baths. Likewise some Irish women also visited the public baths but most managed to make alternative arrangements like visiting a friend that may have purchased their own property or perhaps use the landlady's bath.

Yes, most men would be ready for a good soaking to wash off any bits of concrete, sweat or anything else that had accumulated since the previous Sunday. Peeling backs from sun burn in the hot summer weather necessitated washing off the loose skin that caused discomfort and itch. Sunday morning at the public baths was usually busy and sometimes it was necessary to form a queue. It was two shillings for a towel and soap for our once a week treat. When one was allocated a cubicle the hot water was controlled from the outside by an attendant and the amount of hot water was limited for each bath and if one ran too much cold water it wasn't possible to get more hot water to reheat it. The only alternative would be to queue again for another bath. There was always another alternative to avoid the hassle of queuing by giving a couple of bob to the attendant and one could get all the water and towels required. It wouldn't be Cussons Imperial Leather or even the good old Carbolic soap but soft white Sunlight soap for washing clothes, but it was possible to work up a good odourless lather and one felt better after a good wash.

During the winter months as the weather got colder, visits to public baths became very infrequent. If one overstayed their allotted time in the bath I believe the attendant had the facility to release the bath water but I was never in that situation. I often think of the young generation of today who feel it necessary to shower and wash their hair every morning. Of course it is the modern, hygienic way to live in the twenty first century but the contrast between a once-a-week bath back in the 1950s and today's every morning shower is a major departure and a step forward from the bad old days. It was very uncomfortable working in dusty sweaty conditions regardless of one's employment but particularly in the construction industry. In warm weather conditions, men returning to their rented accommodation and sharing a room with a few others was far from ideal for everybody concerned. Some might wash their feet in a basin or bucket of water but of course that didn't suffice for a bath or shower. Many suffered from sweat rashes and other sores and diseases due to lack of proper washing facilities, particularly when working with cement. Body sores and rashes were common due to lack of proper washing facilities and wearing clothes contaminated with cement, diesel, oil and chemicals.

One Sunday morning a Kerry man called Tadgh, who shared accommodation with me in Bathurst Gardens decided he'd come along to the baths. It was his first visit but it proved to be a rather bad experience. It was busy so we had to queue but eventually we each got a cubicle. Tadgh put his trousers across the top of the partition between his cubicle and the one adjacent. A chap nicked his trousers and of course it left him in a very difficult predicament. After some time he emerged rather distressed wrapped in a big bath towel. He said, '*I've lost my trousers. Could you go back to our room and fetch me another as quickly as possible.*' I headed back to our room in Bathurst Gardens as fast as I could and got a replacement. Apparently trouser nicking was a regular occurrence generally perpetrated by youths and the reason was to search pockets for money or other valuables. Tadgh lost his money and his watch as he had taken it off and put it in his trouser pocket before going into the bath. That Sunday night his mates had a whip round at his local pub to get him enough money to help him to buy food through the following week 'till he got his wages.

Many men, at some time or another, slept rough. The reason that some men slept rough was they'd have been thrown out by a number of landladies for damping down (bed wetting) and sometimes worse. Many had weak kidneys from heavy drinking over a number of years. A few landlords and landladies catered for such men by converting an old garage or outbuilding into a kind of big room to accommodate up to four men. They would put mattresses on the floor and they'd have the use of an outside toilet, but they wouldn't have any cooking facilities so it would have to be full board. It was a rough way to live, but better than sleeping out in the open.

For men sharing double beds where their bed partner was

damping down it would be necessary to use the brown polish plan to get rid of him. Some would put lumps of brown polish on the sheet and then smear a bit of it here and there on the dampers side. That always ensured that he'd be evicted that day. When landladies were making beds and removed the bed covers, if they saw brown on the sheets they wouldn't examine it but roll up the sheet and prepare to evict the man that slept on that side of the bed.

Another problem with having a bed partner would be that some nights he'd arrive back late from the pub. He may be intoxicated and be bothered with a bit of flatulence and would sometimes blow off at high pressure. It could be very unsettling and unhygienic sharing a bed with somebody like that. It often started a fight throughout the night and more often than not the wind breaker would be evicted next morning. Another despicable habit particularly for non-smokers was sharing a room with somebody that smoked particularly late at night. Word would get round about people like that and it would prove difficult for them to get accommodation; hence sleeping rough would be the only alternative. Some landladies would have men sharing beds with complete strangers. They would try to maximise profits by whatever means possible even having men sleeping in the attic.

Another reason for sleeping rough was that some men wanted to have the reputation of being hard men or they liked the title of a 'Long Distance Man'. Long Distance Men were men that couldn't settle anywhere except for short periods. They were good workers but the call of the open road meant they'd only stay in a town or city for short periods. Having only worked a couple of days on a construction site if the urge came to go, I suppose it could be described as a bit like an urge to go to the toilet, they'd down tools and they were off. They'd be away to the next town or wherever. They liked the freedom of the open road and found it difficult being tied down in a construction site. They'd sometimes sleep rough under hedges, bridges or out-houses as they would have bed wetting problems. Some of the Long Distance Men that worked in a couple of construction sites that I worked in would be reluctant to talk about their place of origin or in some cases even about Ireland..

They would have a little bag with their few bits and pieces.

Some were big strong men but gradually years of tramping from place to place took its toll. Some would be getting unemployment benefit or perhaps something similar but how they'd qualify in the absence of a permanent address was a bit of a mystery. Of course, they'd get a few pounds for short periods that they would work and also get a few pounds from some generous Irish people on site or sometimes in the pub. However, it was a kind of a day to day existence and a type of hardship that only a certain type of person could endure. It was a nomadic lifestyle.

It was a rather lonely life in that they would have lost contact with any family that they had through years of non-communication. Sometimes they would have a wash in public conveniences or on the construction site where they worked but clean fresh clothing would be a problem as they worked and slept in the clothes they were wearing. They had their own group of friends or acquaintances and usually knew their whereabouts. It was a bit like a regiment, but they were liked by most of their fellow countrymen. They visited certain pubs that were frequented by their friends. On occasions it would be possible to meet the same men on a site in south Wales or the North of Scotland. The sad thing was that after years of moving and tramping about they would end up in poor health and penniless in some old doss house where nobody bothered about them.

There is a story about a man who slept rough in a field one night and as a result caught a very severe cold. He explained how a number of other men were also sleeping in the same field and that the last man that came into the field late at night left the gate open. He said that there was a terrible draught all night and that was how he caught the cold!

Some of the greedy landladies were happy to have heavy drinkers provided they didn't damp down or worse. Most heavy drinkers wouldn't have breakfast in the morning or return at night for dinner, so that saved the landlady money. To make things look authentic she'd bring a cooked breakfast to the table which she had cooked for one of the regular breakfast eaters, but who had yet to consume it and offer it to a man she knew wouldn't have anything to eat. Usually all they wanted was a cup of tea. She'd then take the cooked breakfast back to the kitchen and put it in the cooker oven to keep it hot but she'd mutter, '*What a waste I'll have to throw that in the garbage bin.*' These men couldn't accuse her of paying for breakfast and not getting it. Some landladies were up to all the dodges.

In rented accommodation some landladies would charge men to retain their rooms while they went on holiday to Ireland or elsewhere for a few weeks. As soon as the men vacated their rooms the landlady would rent them out again to others for the holiday period. On the other hand, Irish women didn't have the same domestic problems as their men counterparts. Shopping, cooking and cleaning were chores that they were accustomed to before they left home. They'd return to their accommodation at a reasonable time as most worked the day shift. Also they wouldn't cook big amounts of food like their male counterparts as most factories had subsidised canteens.

19.
Daily Life

Breakfast in the morning for many Irishmen would be a visit to a café adjacent to the site and in some cases 'twas also a visit to a café in the evening for a bite of dinner. For others it would be straight to the pub to drink the dinner - a kind of liquid dinner. Some preferred a bit of onsite rough cooking and it was called *'rustling up a bit of a shackle up'*. Various cooking utensils would be used such as a big cast iron frying pan which was rarely cleaned and burned black, or the square mouth shovel washed clean and shiny and then placed on top of a lighted propane gas ring. The men would visit a local butchers and purchase best frying steak, sausages, eggs and mushrooms. Lamb chops were another favourite for some of the heavy squad's morning menu. The lovely smell of steak and onions cooking out in the open was rather appetising but not approved of by some of our English friends.

Some sites also used coke fires for cooking purposes. The coke was burned in a brazier or an old drum with holes round the sides but it emitted a lot of fumes. When it was considered that the pan or shovel was hot enough, a big lump of cooking fat would be applied and steak and onions or steak and sausages cooked on it. When cooked some men would take a pork chop with both hands and eat it off the bone. Eating the chop was a bit like playing a mouth organ in that they moved it back and forth across their mouths eating off the bone. For some the enjoyable bit would be grease running down both sides of their mouth.

When the meal was finished it was back to work digging with the square mouth shovel that had just fried some steak. It was a multi-purpose tool. Some might prefer boiled eggs and yes, something to boil them in may be a problem but while there's a will there's a way. After the tea was made the kettle became the favourite cooking utensil for boiling eggs and sometimes it may be loaded up with up to a dozen eggs. Cutlery was a rather scarce commodity on some sites so it would be necessary to improvise. A pen knife or a hacksaw blade would be used to cut a loaf of bread or even a pick to open a tin of beans. These are things I saw with my own eyes. The kettle was also used to heat up beans or even heat up tins of soup. They'd open a tin of beans, take the lid off the kettle and drop the tin on to the bottom which contained some boiling water. It would be the same procedure to heat a tin of soup. The kettle became a multi-purpose cooking utensil also. All the above was what they called - '*a shackle up on site*'. They used to say that when they got a good '*tightner*' (feed) in the morning it set them up for the day and sometimes substituted for the evening meal.

Most of the heavies liked bacon, cabbage and plenty of murphy's (potatoes). Camden Town and Shepherd's Bush were two locations that had café's catering for that traditional Irish grub but they were pretty basic and some were either Irish owned or Irish staffed. The order would often be bacon, cabbage and plenty Kerr Pinks and make sure the bacon has a good rim of fat. Although the cafés were a bit basic they served good generous portions and weren't expensive. Some liked steak, onions, mushrooms and spuds washed down with the black stuff but others would have tea or milk. Of course the café's didn't sell Guinness but anybody that liked a drink of it with their grub took a bottle or two from the pub and glasses would be made available in the café. Some were regular daily customers who'd also have breakfast and dinner at weekends.

I recall a rather sad occasion on a contract that I worked in outside Exeter in Devon. Dennis from Kerry got news that his brother died suddenly in Kerry. He was in a bit of a state as he didn't have the fare to go home. The site ganger contacted the contractor and explained the situation. He (the contractor) generously paid the return boat fare to Ireland and the men on site had a collection to help with expenses. The contractor also arranged for a William Press vehicle to take Dennis to London to catch the train for Holyhead for the boat. It had taken his family in Kerry a couple of days to trace his whereabouts as communication was rather poor in the early 1960s but I think that he had a brother living in Birmingham who eventually tracked him down through contacts in London.

Many Irish men and women worked in Heinz 57 Soup Variety factory and Wall's Sausage factory in Harlesden. In one accommodation I shared a room with a Limerick man called Thomas Power who was working at Walls Sausage factory. His wage was £7 per week net. Out of that he saved £3 per week and sent it back to Limerick on a monthly basis to be put in the Bank of Ireland. His brother had worked and lived in London since the late 1940s so he paid Thomas's fare to London. Even if he saved £3 every week for 52 weeks it would only amount to £156. He went to London in 1951 at the age of 22. He said that he'd return home to Limerick when he had saved £1000. He didn't smoke, drink or have holidays. Saving at the rate of £156 per year would take almost seven years to save £1000. His mission was to renovate his old home and live with his mother. Over a five years period prior to leaving home Thomas estimated that his income for that period was less than £100. He would work with farmers for a few weeks during the summer period saving hay for £1 per day but he didn't always get paid. It demonstrates how values have changed over the past sixty years.

Others worked for London Transport and many women worked in hospitals nursing. Many Irishmen purchased their own property, either terraced or semi-detached houses. They'd work hard for a period of time and save enough to pay a deposit. To help pay the mortgage they'd rent out the top floor which usually consisted of a few rooms, toilet and sometimes a kitchen. The bathroom was usually downstairs in the ground floor, but only for the use of the landlady and landlord. Some landlords provided a bathroom upstairs but most didn't want to lose a bedroom as it meant lost rent revenue. Others didn't have a kitchen but a cooker situated on the landing for everybody's use. Some wouldn't bother cooking so it took some of the pressure off those who did. It could end up in arguments from time to time about having to wait to get the use of the cooker, also for not cleaning up spills, overflows and leaving the cooker dirty. Of course that wasn't always the case but it did occur from time to time particularly with people arriving back late from work and in a hurry to get back out again to meet friends or maybe the long-haired mate.

Sunday morning wouldn't be the same without a trip to Petticoat Lane. It was a famous London market that many Irishmen and women visited. It was possible to purchase inexpensive clothing and shoes particularly for working in the construction and utilities industries. However, one had to be careful about the quality of some of the merchandise. A room-mate purchased some teaspoons and took them back to our accommodation. We duly made tea and used the new spoons but when they were put into the hot tea they did a *'Uri Geller'* - so clearly not fit for purpose or value for money.

A trip to Hyde Park, sometimes called Speakers Corner was another Sunday must. It had some entertaining characters like Old George who usually spoke about World War11. He used to say people were told, *'If you see a bomb drop catch it.'* In very warm weather some people cooled off by having a dip in the Serpentine. It was also a place to meet friends from home and catch up on the latest news. Laundry for most was a bit of a problem particularly for men working six days per week. Laundries would be closed by the time they returned to their accommodation on most evenings. Some of the better landladies would help by taking the washing to the laundry and collecting it. The only laundry most Irishmen would have were shirts and socks. How times have changed from the 1940s, '50s and '60s in that many Irishmen during that era didn't wear underpants, pyjamas or a house coat. Most slept in the buff.

In the evening by the time the food was cooked and eaten it was time to go to bed. Although for most Irishmen working in the construction industry it was more flexible to self-cater than to be in digs so far as meals were concerned. Some men would go straight to the pub and remain there 'till closing time. They wouldn't bother cooking or perhaps washing at that time of night but go straight into bed. For some it was a rough lonely life.

For many the new found wealth was life changing but not to everybody's benefit. Being paid on a weekly basis meant that some men lavished their money on drink and gambling. The transition from living in Ireland without any weekly income to suddenly have a weekly wage and permanent employment was just too much to handle. Dog tracks were popular at that time and many lost a lot of money gambling at Wembley Greyhound Stadium and White City which were both popular dog venues. Before going to place bets on dogs at the above venues many were well topped up with drink.

The Greyhound pub near Wembley Stadium was a popular watering hole on the way to the Stadium. Some men would go into the Greyhound pub on their way home from work and have quite a few drinks before going to the Stadium. On occasions some would lose all their money at the Stadium and they'd then borrow money from their colleagues. For the men that had lost their money it would have to be a sub next day at their place of employment to pay back the money they had borrowed and have money to buy food. Drink and dogs became a way of life for many and the new found wealth ended in disaster. It was sad to see good, hard working men getting addicted to drink and gambling and throwing away their hard earned money. Horse racing was another source of gambling that drained resources. It would sometimes result in not having proper meals, not keeping their accommodation clean and tidy and resulted in eviction. As the drinking and gambling took hold many Irishmen finished up without a roof over their head. However, some men were pretty domesticated and kept their accommodation clean and tidy and cooked good meals.

That was life for some of the Irish emigrants living in London back in the 1950s and 1960s. I must say the men that I worked with on most utility contracts were strong healthy people and the rough way of life didn't have any adverse effects on them. Everything that I have stated above is one hundred per cent correct and the rough way of life that I experienced didn't have any adverse effect on me apart from the Asian flu, a poisoned hand and a bit of steel in my left eye.

20.
Fashion Trends, Relaxation and Recreation

B ack in the 1950s Irishmen in London weren't renowned for fashion and that included me. Trousers with twenty eight or thirty inch bottoms with turn ups and double breasted jackets were the order of the day. It mostly applied to men from the west and south of Ireland. Two drapers' shops in Harlesden that Irishmen frequented were Scott's and Harrington's. My draper's shop was Harringtons and usually they were pretty good. I had, however, one rather bad experience where they got measurements mixed up. I was about to go home on holiday for Christmas and I went to collect my suit. *'Yes your suit is ready.'* I was told by the gentleman that was serving. I tried it on and it was about ten sizes too big for me. They had measured a number of people for suits the day that I ordered mine and unfortunately put the incorrect measurements against my name. When I came out of the changing room I was like the Michelin X man. They were unable to alter it and they didn't have the time to make me a new one. However, they offered to make me a new suit free of charge but it wouldn't be ready until I got back from my holidays.

Irishmen didn't usually buy off the peg suits as the preference was made to measure. Most men were rather bulky and felt that off the peg suits would be rather skimpy on their bulky frames. It was a busy time for drapers in the run up to Christmas in that many Irishmen returned home for the festive season and they wanted to look their best. Trousers with twenty eight and thirty inch bottoms with turn- ups and double breasted jackets took a lot of material and it made them that bit more expensive. The trousers looked very untidy and because sometimes men trailed them along the ground when walking, Cockneys referred to them as street sweepers. Trouser legs and bottoms of this width were in stark contrast to Teddy Boy trousers known as *'drain pipes'*. One trouser leg of twenty eight or thirty inch width and turn-ups would take more material to make than the two legs of a drain pipe trouser. Some liked buttoned up flies and others preferred zips.

Most men were easy to satisfy but some would expect the draper to throw in some extras such as a shirt, a trouser belt or braces in recognition of their continued custom. If the draper was reluctant to throw in a freebee it would be a case of taking their custom elsewhere. Some Irishmen liked to do a bit of wheeling and dealing but drapers soon got wise in the knowledge that some would expect a freebee and take account of that by inflating the price of the suit. The favourite shoe shops were Bata or Freeman Hardy and Willis. Again some would expect a pair of socks or suchlike thrown in. Sometimes after a fight on a Saturday night the winner might explain how he won it by saying, '*I gave him a good kicking in the arse with a pair of Freeman Hardy and Willis.*'

Irishmen returning home would wish to look their best and so would the ladies. For the ladies who hadn't emigrated, men returning home on holiday were always a bit of an attraction particularly at church on Sunday or at the local dance halls. A good application of Brilliantine and a generous splash of the good old Brute would be enough to send most ladies hearts racing. Some families and friends particularly young single adult females struggling to make ends meet on a small holding would be attracted to the rather handsome men folk on holiday from either Britain or America. The attraction would be the rather expensive suits, white shirts with bright colour ties and plenty of money in the hip pocket. Yes, some would look rather prosperous with considerably more cash to splash than before they emigrated.

Likewise ladies would return with expensive clothes, trendy hair styles, high heel shoes and lashings of make-up. Some ladies returning from America would have developed a distinct American accent although they may have only been away for a short period. Allegedly one lady didn't recognise the cat. She asked her mother, '*Oh mother say what is that thing with the great long tail.*' However, most attracted the attention of bachelor farmers who found it difficult to resist the great smell of American perfume although in some cases there were some farmers that would have the great smell of farmyard manure. Some bachelors would be so desperate to get a woman they'd be willing to take one of these lovely ladies without a dowry but having had a taste of life overseas most wouldn't be interested going into a farm.

All this unsettled the ones struggling to survive at home so inevitably they too emigrated although, in some cases, the small holding would have been passed over to them by their parents. Regrettably, when they got to Britain or America the grass wasn't as green as had been portrayed by their friends. They'd regret leaving home but their pride would prevent them from returning as they would be seen as failures. The ones who emigrated thought the brother at home on the farm was the lucky one while he in turn thought the brothers and sisters who emigrated were the lucky ones!

Most socialising in England was done in the Irish dance halls where Irishmen and women went to meet their friends, boyfriends and girlfriends and to exchange any news from home. There were numerous Irish dancehalls in London, Birmingham, Manchester and elsewhere in the 1950s. Some of the Irish dancehalls in London were the Galtymore in Cricklewood, the Bamba in Kilburn High Road, the Garryowen in Hammersmith, the Blarney Club in Tottenham Court Road, the Shamrock in Elephant and Castle, the Round Tower in Holloway Road and the Gresham in Archway. For many they were places of entertainment and for some they brought hope for the future and were also a means to suppress loneliness. The music and atmosphere acted as a kind of stimulus that transported the emigrant back home without actually having to make the journey.

Most Irish dancehalls used to be packed to capacity back in the 1950s with the cream of Ireland's youth of both genders, all hoping to meet their future wife or husband. The girls would be lined up at one side of the dance floor with their cloakroom ticket neatly folded under their watch strap or bracelet. Some would have a handbag but most left their bags in the cloakroom. The men folk would be lined up on the other side. It was an opportunity for both men and women to evaluate and weigh up the opposite sex across the dance floor. Some ladies would be seated, as if they weren't too interested in dancing or boyfriends, but they liked to observe.

The ladies wore long black stockings or skin colour stockings with a seam running up the back. They were secured with some kind of harness to prevent slippage. Some of the dances would involve a bit of rapid swinging. The swinging would reveal some colourful under garments. One night at the Blarney Club, Tottenham Court Road a young lady had a rather embarrassing situation. As she swung with her partner an under garment dropped to her ankles and she got tangled up in it. She fell to the floor bringing her partner down with her. She had to undo some of the harness to remove it before getting back on her feet. She got a very big cheer from just about everybody on the dance floor as well as from members of the band. She made a quick dash to the ladies toilet accompanied by some of her friends to put things back as they were.

Many girls didn't wear makeup but some would give their lips a fairly generous application of red lipstick and they would have a good splash of perfume. Eye shadow and plucked eyebrows hadn't quite hit the market but the cream of Ireland's female youth shone in most Irish dancehalls. Ireland's beautiful young women were in abundance. Some girls had pretty generous eyebrows and a good growth of hair above their upper lip.

Ladies' choice was always popular and an opportunity for some girls to get their man on the floor and chat him up in the hope that he would ask to take her home. Some would be rather disappointed that their man hadn't popped the question. Some girls used to say it gave them the opportunity to ask their man about the number of acres and livestock he left behind in Ireland. When dancehalls were packed to capacity oxygen would be in short supply and without air conditioning they became very unpleasant places.

Some Irishmen were rather shy and found it difficult to pop the question directly. They'd digress a little by asking the question indirectly such as, 'How would you like to be buried with my people?' Or it may be, 'How would you like to be my widow when I die?' Some of the girls were a bit fussy and wary of the boys they danced with especially if they asked to see them home. Many of the girls would do the office test in an effort to evaluate the status of the boyo without asking him. The test would take place when they were dancing in that the girl would explore the palm of his hand for hard skin and welts. If the boyo had welts and hard skin at the base of each finger and the centre of the palm it was a good indication of the type of 'office' that he worked in. Rough hands were a dead giveaway and she could be pretty certain that he didn't work in the Financial District or the Stock Exchange. More often than not they would be Wimpey, Laing or McAlpine's Fusiliers known as *'the heavies'*. However, what the girls didn't seem to realise was the fact that the heavies were on better paid jobs than many office workers. Many men folk would try to impress the ladies by wearing their pioneer pin, although they'd have had a few drinks before entering the dance hall. The hair would get a generous application of Brilliantine or Pomade hair dressing in an attempt to enhance their looks. Yes, most were the cream of Ireland's youth and most had the same thing in common – involuntary immigration from the Emerald Isle.

Some of the men usually got well topped up at a pub adjacent to the dancehall before going in. In some cases they'd top up a bit too much and after the dancehall closed it was fairly common to see the girlfriend with the boyfriend on tow heading for the nearest bus stop. For some it would be necessary to make some emergency stops in shop doorways en route to the bus stop to offload or vomit some of the excess fuel that they didn't burn off on the dance floor. On occasions the girlfriend would have to assist by encouraging the boyfriend to put his finger down his throat to induce sickness and maximise the discharge. After a couple of heaves, one or two almighty roars, a bit of rodding of the throat with his finger and a couple of good thumps on the back from the girlfriend he'd suddenly discharge a gush of Guinness, and an assortment of food and god knows what else might be in the mix.

The second emergency stop would perhaps be only a rumbling or aftershock and wouldn't be as productive as the first. The top shirt button would be undone and the tie pulled down and sideways. He'd blame a *'devil of a bad pint'* that he got at the Spotted Dog, the Greyhound or some other pub and then poor Mary, Eileen, Peggy or whoever would have to clean up the suit and shoes. Having completed the tow job to the bus stop the next problem was getting her lover on the bus. With a bit of assistance from some friends at the bus stop they'd manage to get him on. The next problem was to get him off the bus as he'd be fast asleep by the time that he arrived at the stop nearest his accommodation. Again with a bit of assistance from other passengers they'd manage to get him off. Then the girlfriend would have to complete the tow job to his accommodation. She'd perhaps open the door for him and once she got him inside it was mission complete 'till the next time. Then the poor girlfriend would have to get herself home. Usually the boyfriend takes the girlfriend home but on occasions such as I have described above the girlfriend would end up taking the boyfriend home. Yes, some girlfriends didn't have an easy time as the tow job may have to be repeated most weekends, but it became a way of life.

The vast majority of the men that over indulged on a Saturday night were hard working and gentlemen through and through. It would be a combination of circumstances that caused them to get so intoxicated such as meeting friends that they hadn't seen for a while. Also the craic would be good and the drink flowing with friends buying their rounds too frequently or out of turn. Many didn't want to have the reputation of not being able to keep up with their mates. Inevitably they'd consume too much drink in too short a period. Many Irishmen would scoff at their English friends' inability to consume large amounts of alcohol and particularly the type of alcohol they drank. Englishmen were very moderate in their drinking habits. They could enjoy their night chatting with their friends, supping a half pint of bitter or light ale. They also enjoyed a bit of a sing song or a *'knees up Mother Brown'* sort of thing. They'd go home sober with almost the same amount of money that they left the house with. Yes, there was the odd few who over indulged. It had to be pint measures for Paddy and some of the heavy drinkers could gulp down up to ten pints in one night's drinking session. There were, of course, many moderate drinkers who drank responsibly and also enjoyed their night out.

The difference between social life for Englishmen and Irishmen was that most Irishmen didn't have any commitments or responsibilities. Most Englishmen would have a wife and family to provide for, as well as a mortgage and day-to-day commitments. Most Irishmen were single and lived on a day-to-day week-to-week basis. They liked to compete with each other about the amount of alcohol they could consume over a weekend. Back in the 1950s and 1960s pints of Guinness were Paddy's favourite drink so Arthur Guinness must have been laughing all the way to the bank. Paddy liked a good white head on top of his pint of Guinness. Every time he drank out of the glass he'd have a white moustache on his upper lip.

Pub conversations were mainly about work, dogs and horses and defending the title (fighting). It was a way of life for many Irishmen at that time. Irishmen were renowned for their work performance in the construction and utilities industries, but many had a bad anti-social reputation particularly at weekends. They fought in the pubs, dancehalls, public transport and in the streets, mostly due to excessive drinking. For some it wouldn't be a good weekend if they weren't involved in a fight and locked up by the police. They liked the title of being hard men. However, the excess consumption of alcohol over a number of years together with tobacco abuse resulted in being overweight with lung, kidney and liver failure and consequently dying at a young age.

Communication was sometimes a problem when the boyfriend wished to contact the girlfriend during the week in that she wouldn't have a landline or mobile phone. It would then be a case of writing a note, going to her accommodation and popping it through the letter box. The other means of communication would be a visit to her accommodation and throw small stones at her bedroom window under the cover of darkness or climb a drain pipe adjacent to her window and tap on it. Climbing a drain pipe could be a bit dodgy after a few drinks as a Mayo chap who shared accommodation with me found out. The drain pipe came away from the wall and he fell backwards resulting in a broken leg and he was unable to work for a number of weeks. Yes, life could be difficult for the boyfriend also.

The Irish dance halls in London, Birmingham, Manchester and other cities and towns that had large Irish communities were places to practice and share traditional values in music and dance. Bands such as Joe Loss and his vocalist Rose Brennan and the Malachy Sweeney Ceili Band from County Armagh with vocalist Anna Boyle were nights always to be looked forward to. These bands always had dance halls packed to capacity. The music and song seemed to inject a stimulus, invigorate the blood stream and rekindle their old traditional Irish values. Sadly the above bands became fragmented when key members left to do other things. From memory I think Anna Boyle left the Malachy Sweeney Ceili

Band and went to America. Thereafter the band wasn't the same in her absence.

On a Saturday night they'd be a dance above Burtons the tailors in Cricklewood Broadway, London and many would go there when the Galtymore closed. A bus service was laid on to transport people home in the early hours of Sunday morning to various parts of London. Back in the 1950s London seemed to be a safer place at night to walk about particularly for women.

The weekend was sometimes a time to settle old scores after the pubs closed and it resulted in some getting free transport home or at least part of the way in a black Mariah or sometimes it was referred to as Paddy's taxi. Sunday afternoon was Tea Dance and novelty prize time at the Blarney, Tottenham Court Road. The Palais in Hammersmith and other Irish dance halls were also venues for Sunday afternoon tea dances. All dance halls were lively places and always a good craic especially at weekends.

21.
Irish Weddings

Irish weddings in London and elsewhere were usually happy occasions and a time to celebrate but some did end up in a fight rather than *'Auld Lang Syne'*. Most people would be heavily intoxicated and it would result in an argument about some old score that had to be settled.

I recall a couple of weddings in the Kilburn and Camden Town area's where violence erupted and the groom and some guests spent the first night of the wedding in a police cell. It would be fuelled by drink and would be most embarrassing for the bride and both sets of parents. The regrettable part would be that the groom wouldn't be directly involved but simply acting as a go-between in most cases.

Drinking at the wedding and getting drunk was one thing, but the groom arriving at church too drunk to get married was something else that happened on a couple of occasions. I never witnessed such an occasion but allegedly there was one such case in Camden Town and another in Holloway Road. Apparently the grooms arrived at church but were unable to speak so therefore unable to partake in the marriage ceremony. The weddings had to be postponed and the people that arrived at church with presents went home again. It was most embarrassing for the brides to be and indeed for both sets of parents. Allegedly the Camden Town wedding never took place but I don't know if the Holloway Road wedding went ahead later.

Most wedding receptions were held in pubs in an upstairs area specially set aside for such occasions, but some would be wrecked before the end of the night. Weddings back in the 1950s and early 1960s weren't as lavish as todays, but nevertheless a time for celebration.

Some guests would travel from Ireland, such as parents and other family members of the bride and groom. For parents that couldn't be with their loved one on the big day it was a rather sad occasion for them. My wedding in Scotland in 1962 was in the absence of both my parents. My dad had passed away in 1952 and my mother wasn't able to travel that far. I know that it was difficult for her at home in County Clare and all the more difficult in that we couldn't communicate. Mobile phones weren't heard of at that time and she didn't have a landline.

For parents that made the journey to the UK to be with their loved ones it could be quite an ordeal as it would be their first time away from home. Arriving in London or some other big city or town was like landing on another planet. Endeavouring to communicate with some English guests could be another ordeal for many. It wouldn't be possible to have an instant cultural exchange! Leaving the Irish countryside and arriving in London was quite a shock to the system.

On the morning of the wedding, guests would arrive at church carrying a large brown paper parcel. It would contain the wedding present and at that time it was usually sheets or blankets or both. They were very popular presents back in that era. Duvets hadn't hit the market or maybe they weren't popular, but I don't recall anybody giving duvets as a wedding present. Other presents may be a canteen of cutlery, an ironing board or a lampshade. It sometimes ended up a bit like the Brendan Grace wedding with multiple ironing boards and lampshades. In those days they didn't have a show of presents prior to the wedding for the following reasons. Presents were usually given to the couple either at church on the morning of the wedding or later at the reception and in some cases it may be weeks later before all presents were received. Another reason was that both the bride and groom would be living in rented accommodation prior to the wedding.

Sometimes a wedding present could turn out to be rather disappointing for the recipient and highly embarrassing for the person who gave it. One bride got a canteen of cutlery as a present from a friend nicely wrapped with a card stuck on the outside. However, when the bride opened it she found a card inside the canteen of cutlery with her sister's name and signature on it! It emerged that the canteen of cutlery was a present which her sister had given to the mutual friend a couple of years prior to the occasion of this wedding. Red faces all around!

Nevertheless, most weddings were happy occasions and the start of a new life for the bride and groom away from their native land. For many it was a case of living in rented accommodation for a while after their marriage until they'd manage to save enough for a deposit on a property of their own. Some wouldn't have a honeymoon in England. Some would return home to the parents in Ireland, especially if the parents had not managed to attend the wedding. For some parents it would be an opportunity to meet their daughter-in-law or son-in-law for the first time and give them the once over. It would be a great occasion for the parents concerned, especially if they hadn't seen their son or daughter for a number of years. Everything would have to be spick and span for the new daughter-in-law or son-in-law and that meant painting and whitewashing inside and out.

The next hurdle for the newlyweds would be attending their local church particularly their first Sunday in the neighbourhood. It would be necessary to introduce their partner to friends and neighbours. Standing outside the church would be a great opportunity for the neighbours to do a full evaluation of the newlyweds and make appropriate or inappropriate comments as was usually the case. In 1962 I took my new wife to Ireland, for the first time, for our honeymoon. As explained earlier my wedding was in Scotland and my brother and sister made the journey. When we arrived in County Clare my mother met my Scottish wife for the first time. It was a bit difficult at first for my mother with a broad Clare accent to communicate with my wife with her broad Scottish accent and vice versa. My mother and sister did a lot of work in preparation for our homecoming such as painting and whitewashing the house. I always remember they cleared out a little room and made it into a dining area. They were both so very good.

Neighbours came to the house to wish us well so we enjoyed our honeymoon. However, my first Sunday at Lissycasey church was an occasion for friends and neighbours to evaluate the newlyweds from Scotland, particularly my wife. Some comments about my wife that a neighbour overheard were – '*I'd say she wouldn't be much good footing turf in the bog.*' '*Jaysus I'd say she never milked a cow in her life*' and '*I wonder what she thinks of the Lissycasey people.*' At that time it was rather unusual for somebody from a farming community to marry a person from another country. Anyhow all went well and Sunday number two at church was less stressful, but still some were anxious to know a bit more.

For those who couldn't afford a honeymoon some landlords or landladies were helpful and generous. I lived in rented accommodation in Wood Green, London towards the end of the 1950s. A Kerry chap who had lived there for a number of years got married, but couldn't afford to have a honeymoon as he had been off work for a period of time through an accident, prior to his wedding. The landlord was a Mayo man and he made his house available free of charge for the newlyweds to have a bit of a party and a get together with their parents on the night of their wedding. He arranged accommodation for me and a few others with some of his family and friends for the night. The newlyweds had a party and their parents stayed overnight which meant that they didn't have to pay for accommodation. On other occasions similar arrangements for newlyweds were made in Kilburn and Shepherds Bush areas; so there were some decent landlords and landladies on occasions such as I've described.

I was best man in London on three occasions back in the late 1950s early 1960s. I recall a London wedding at which I was only a guest and where things didn't go smoothly on the morning of the wedding. The best man, who was the groom's brother, had put his suit into the cleaners and forgot to collect it. He dashed to the cleaners but they were closed and didn't open 'till late morning. His brother had to give him one of his old suits. He was a good bit bulkier and a bit taller than his brother so he had to squeeze into the groom's old suit. The trouser legs were about two inches above the top of his shoes. The jacket was about ten sizes too small for him. It looked a bit like a Laurel and Hardy wedding and some family members were rather embarrassed. After the service he collected his own suit from the cleaners and then went on to the reception. At the reception the groom explained to the guests what had happened but it was embarrassing nonetheless.

22.
Some Funny and Not so Funny Experiences

In my accommodation in Harlesden North London, which I referred to earlier, there were two brothers from East Clare and they were both lovely people. The landlord Jimmy Darcy and his wife were also lovely people and looked after us very well. They took our washing to the laundry and collected it and also kept our rooms tidy and clean. I mention the brothers as they had a bit of an experience with Mrs Darcy's cat. At the weekend they'd cook a leg of lamb for sandwiches to take to work. It wasn't the case that Mrs Darcy didn't feed her cat well, but he was partial to a bit of lamb. One Sunday night the cooked leg of lamb was left on a plate on top of the cooker and it was too much temptation for the cat to resist. He climbed onto the cooker and pulled the lamb and plate onto the floor. He was a bit fussy in that he ate the more edible bits and left the rest scattered around the floor. He didn't like overcooked lamb it seems. The plate became a number of pieces!

On the Monday morning when the younger of the two brothers entered the kitchen the cat was lying on the floor a bit bloated looking like he had over indulged. The older brother also entered the kitchen and seeing the remnants of the leg of lamb he became pretty irate saying, '*The so & so cat is bursting to go out for a s..t, I'll let him out.*' He then went downstairs in his bare feet with the cat following behind. He opened the downstairs kitchen door leading onto the back garden. It was his intention to get a kick at the cat as he made his exit but missed and struck the door jam instead with his toes. He came back upstairs and looked out the window. He said to his younger brother, '*Look out at the f....n cat trying to get rid of our lamb.*' Later on they saw the funny side of it and had a good laugh.

On another occasion a friend of mine called Johnny and I decided to look for other accommodation and rented a room off the Harrow Road near Kensal Rise. Soon after taking occupancy we went to Ireland on holiday and returned on a Saturday. I sourced some food to restock our cupboard and I purchased a piece of boiling beef. The cooker was situated on the landing upstairs. I put the beef onto boil with approximately two pounds of onions, carrot and parsnip, on what I thought was a low gas but not low enough. Johnny and I went to bed to get some sleep in the afternoon as we had been travelling all night and we intended going to the Galtymore dancehall that night. The window on the landing was half open and yes, the smoke was belching out. The beef was burning and a neighbour phoned the fire service. Everybody else in the building was out shopping, as was usually the case on a Saturday afternoon. When the fire service arrived they couldn't gain entry so they broke down the front door. They got us out of bed and of course we were in a state of shock. They took the burnt pot and beef outside but thankfully the house wasn't damaged apart from a bit of smoke damage. We contacted the proprietors and explained what had happened and offered to pay for the damage, but they claimed on their insurance. After that we didn't leave anything that was cooking unattended.

I don't recall any accommodation that had central heating back in the 1950s era. It was usually a paraffin heater and they could be dangerous, especially if they were toppled over. Also the fumes could be harmful when they weren't serviced at regular intervals. I can recall two incidents with paraffin heaters, one in Harlesden and one in Willesden. The one in Harlesden resulted in a fire when the heater was overturned. The house was badly damaged but everybody got out unharmed. The incident in Willesden was associated with fumes. A gentleman returned after a night out and he put the heater on, fell asleep and was overcome by fumes. Allegedly the heater wasn't serviced and it was emitting fumes. He was fortunate in that his room-mate found him in an unconscious state when he returned after a night out. He was taken to hospital for treatment and luckily survived.

23.
Local Watering Holes

It was a bit of a shock for many arriving in a British city or town but almost all towns and cities in the UK had significant numbers of Irishmen and women who formed Irish communities. It never fully compensated for the homeland, but it was of great significance to meet up in pubs or places of entertainment and meet people from home to catch up on the latest news. Some of Ireland's finest men would be packed into pubs in London, Birmingham, Manchester and elsewhere throughout Britain. For many it would be the pub after finishing work; so life was pretty rough for some.

The favourite watering holes (pubs) as described earlier in the Harlesden area were the Crown, the Junction, the Royal Oak and the College. Other pubs in London where the Irish congregated in numbers were the Spotted Dog in Willesden, the Brighton in Camden Town, the Crown in Cricklewood, The Archway Tavern in Archway and the Hop Holes in Hammersmith, to name but a few.

Pub conversations for most men were usually centred round work, the various contractors that they were working for and the rates per shift they were paying. Others might discuss what contractors were paying on measured work and ask *'What's the digging like.'* If the conversation wasn't about work perhaps the subject would be about fighting and men being locked up. It might be about a fight outside a pub or a dancehall the previous night. It would be, *'Did you hear about the fight last night outside the Crown in Cricklewood? There was a 'rake' of men going 'to town' and the 'Johnny Gallagher's' took a load away in a Black Mariah and locked them up. Sure Jaysus they were all well steamed up.'* Other sayings such as *'The horse so and so and the quare one is away to the auld Dart for a couple of weeks,'* Not very often would one be addressed by one's name so instead it would be *'How's it goin' horse.'* or *'How are you doin' scan.'* or *'How is she cuttin' horse. Where are you dogging it out now* (working).' Some Irishmen seemed to talk in a kind of coded language. At weekends most men would be well dressed in their blue serge suits and generous padded jacket shoulders. Many felt that the padded shoulders enhanced their body frame making it a bit bulkier. The herringbone pattern was another favourite back in the 1950s.

Some liked to defend the title (fight) most weekends and it could result in being locked up from the Saturday night 'till Monday morning and then a court appearance. Sometimes it may result in a fine and a lost day's wages. Strange to say but there was the odd one that liked to carry that kind of reputation in that they thought it gave them some prominence.

At that time many pub landlords and bar staff operated various dodges to relieve poor Paddy of his hard earned cash. After a heavy weekend on the booze, Monday for some Irishmen wouldn't be a particularly good day for the office. A bit like New Year resolutions, sometimes Monday morning was a time for some Irishmen to make their resolution. It might be, '*Jaysus 'tis time a man copped himself on, sure that ould bloody drink every weekend wouldn't lave you a penny. Next weekend I'll be on orange juice myself and to hell with the beer. Ah sure Jaysus when a man is steamed up he's buying bloody drink for everybody in the pub and then on a Monday morning nothing in the pockets but an empty fag packet and the lining. Ah sure* Jaysus '*tis a mugs game.*' That was the kind of conversation I often heard and the word Jaysus was frequently used. Although well intentioned when the next weekend came the Monday morning resolution would be broken so it would have to be renewed again the following week and so on.

When pubs were busy, the craic going strong and the loud music playing as a bit of a distraction, some bar staff would fiddle poor old Paddy's change particularly barmaids. This wasn't exclusive to the Harlesden area or London but pretty widespread throughout the UK. The weekend was a time when many men got paid in the pub by the sub- contractor that they were working for. It was an arrangement between many sub-contractors and pub landlords to pay men in the pub. It could be described as exploitation by both contractor and pub landlord. This type of arrangement suited the landlord because his pub would be packed to capacity with men spending money on drink. Likewise it suited the sub-contractor in that the pub became his office at no cost to him and he'd get some free drink from the landlord.

Another racket that was operated in some pubs was cashing cheques. Some contractors paid by cheque and as most Irishmen didn't have a bank or post office account, some pub landlords cashed cheques but charged a significant fee for doing so. Again it would be an arrangement between contractor and pub landlord. Of course in most cases the whole of the cheque value became the property of the pub landlord in the course of a weekend. Some wouldn't get the total cheque value at the time of cashing it in. The landlord would say, '*I can only give you some just now but remind me later and I'll give you the balance.*' It gave poor Paddy time to get fully primed with drink and kept him in the premises drinking 'till he got the balance later on in the evening. However, the balance by that time would be in the landlord's till and poor Paddy could forget about it. Pub landlords would be quid's in, taking into account what they charged for cashing the cheque and the other dodges they got up to.

Flush with money albeit for short periods some liked to impress certain barmaids that took their eye. Sometimes landlords would have decoy barmaids specifically primed up to lure young Irishmen to their pub. These barmaids would be everybody's girlfriend and on many occasions men fought over a barmaid who was only playing to the gallery. Paddy would be seated on a high stool at the bar and when paying for drinks he'd like to impress a particular barmaid by flashing a wad of notes. He'd hand over a twenty pound note when a note of a lesser denomination would suffice and offer to buy her a drink. She'd thank him saying, '*I'll have it later I'm too busy just now.*' Usually she would be the friendly, talkative, and well endowed type of girl in areas where it mattered. What the gentleman wouldn't realise was that she'd have a couple of other admirers further down the bar or perhaps seated at a table also buying her drink for perhaps the same reason. It may be possible that she wouldn't have a drink all night but collect the money from the change before she handed it over to her various admirers. The money retained would be the price of an exotic drink rather than a glass of ale! She'd be happy with what she collected and her admirers would be happy with their night's viewing but it would have been rather costly.

Many pubs that had large concentrations of Irish customers and Irish bar staff were prone to fiddling, particularly just towards closing time. It would sometimes be difficult to get served after last orders were shouted. There would be a rush for the bar and people would be pushing and shoving endeavouring to buy a last round. In most cases it wouldn't be necessary to buy any more drink as tables would be loaded with full pints of Guinness, lager and glasses of all types of spirits. When a ten or twenty pound note was handed over to a member of bar staff to pay for drinks they'd never count out one's change but hand it over in a lump sum. They'd try to give as many single pound notes as possible to bulk it up and loads of coins. Whoever would be in such an intoxicated state at that time of night wouldn't bother to count the change. He'd roll it up in a bundle, coins and all and put it in his pocket sometimes dropping paper money on the floor. The bar staff would take the correct change out of the till but keep as much as a fiver out of the change of a twenty pound note. Before leaving the pub some would need to visit the toilet to vomit off some of the excess fuel and he might need something out of his trouser pocket such as a handkerchief and in the process would also pull out some paper money and drop it on the floor making it an even more expensive night.

Next day when he'd have sobered up he'd do a quick audit of what money he had left and be shocked at what he thought he had spent the night before. He wouldn't have any idea of what he may have dropped on the floor. He'd say, *'Jaysus I think I was done. I didn't get the right change last night from that so and so barman.'* it would be too late to go back and complain to the member of bar staff concerned.

Short changing happened in most pubs and regrettably it would be Irish staff doing it to their own countrymen and sometimes their own country women, particularly at weekends when pubs would be packed. Some bar staff would make a good week's wages in a night short changing and overcharging their customers. They would overcharge for rounds of drinks, but give the correct change and pocket the amount that they had overcharged. Some men wouldn't know what the total should be for a big round of drinks especially when it was a mixture of beer and spirits. On the odd occasion where discrepancies in change became apparent, it would be difficult to get any satisfaction from the bar staff. It might result in an argument and a shouting match between a member of staff and a customer. On some occasions a customer who was well-fuelled up might become abusive and get thrown out and barred altogether. It didn't happen very often to Irish women as they wouldn't visit the bar with as much regularity.

Some landlords had their own dodges of giving short measures of spirits and adding water to beer particularly when everybody was well fuelled up. A Dublin chap who was a bar man whom I once lived with told me that some landlords would collect full pints of Guinness and other drinks after the pub closed and put them back in their respective barrels in the cellar. He said that was often the reason people got flat pints of Guinness or light ale.

Irishmen tended to congregate outside the pubs when they closed. The police always tried to move them on. Some would become abusive and inevitably it led to arrests. There were some very strong Irishmen and it might take five policemen to arrest one man. I recall one night in Harlesden three policemen trying to arrest a man who was a wrestler, and he broke free. He ran up Nicol Road and jumped into the Catholic Church grounds pursued by the police. They tried once again to arrest him but he knocked two of them to the ground and they were injured. The third policeman attended to his colleagues and the gentleman that they were trying to arrest escaped. He took refuge in a pub that he used to frequent. At that time some Irishmen battled with the police rather than being arrested.

It was in the pub we drank the sub
We drank it with good cheer
But now that it is Monday again
Well damn and f... the beer.

24.
Return to the Emerald Isle

Once in another country it was indeed the case that many emigrants didn't see their parents or other family members again for a number of reasons. People who emigrated to America, Australia or even Britain in some cases could not be contacted when a family member was seriously ill or passed away. There were a number of reasons why people couldn't be contacted. In that type of situation, for a family member in Great Britain who was contactable, it was so much easier for him or her to return home as opposed to somebody who had emigrated to America, Canada or Australia. Communication back in the '40s, '50s and '60s was rather limited in that it was mostly confined to letter writing. Others were unable to return because they didn't have the funds to cover the cost of travel back to the homeland. They may have changed their address or perhaps they may be in hospital and unfit to travel. One of the biggest problems at that time was the use of aliases, which made it even more difficult to locate a person at a time of bereavement.

Irish emigrants in the UK were always willing to help fellow emigrants who had financial problems at a time of bereavement. They'd have pub collections or collections at the workplace and in some cases Irish contractors would make a contribution.

Most Irishmen worked hard and were always in employment and for many it was their intention to return to Ireland when their bank balance looked healthy enough. For most it didn't happen! They met their long term future partner and then along came the family and with other commitments, so going home to Ireland became more and more remote as the years passed by. The longer that people delayed the decision to return home the less likely it became. However, some did return home but for most the original trip was on a one way ticket.

It was 1956 that I and my friend Joe RIP another Lissycasey man decided to return home for a holiday. To get about with a bit of independence it was necessary to have a car. I couldn't drive and my friend Joe just had a few driving lessons from a friend of his. I didn't have a driving licence but I soon got one. At that time all that was required was to complete an application form for a full driving licence. I visited the Courthouse in Ennis and completed the application form and before leaving the building I was handed my licence and both Joe and I headed for Limerick to hire a car. We hired a Volkswagen Beetle from Sarsfield Car Rentals. Joe took the keys and went to an adjacent side street where the car was parked between two other cars. Joe was in the pilot's seat! He couldn't find reverse and on each attempt the car moved a bit forward until it was so close to the car in front that it wasn't possible to make any further attempts to find reverse. I went upstairs to Mr Kirwan the owner and told him about the problem. He said, *'Ah don't worry about it we get lots of people who find it difficult to find reverse gear in a Beetle, I'll come down and show you.'* The gear lever had a flat top and all that was necessary was to push it down and push the lever to the left hand side. After stalling the engine a few times we managed to get out of the city. When we got to a quiet stretch of road Joe showed me the ropes so to speak.

Just south of Clarecastle I was driving but in a low gear and we were approaching a bend and right on the bend was a donkey and cart and I overtook right on the bend. My friend Joe nearly had a heart attack and said that I should have waited behind the slow moving transport as we could both have been killed had something been coming towards us. I pulled over and Joe went back into the driving seat!

He drove for the rest of that day and things were okay 'till it was getting dark and time for lights. It took him some time to find the light switch but when he found it he only had the parking lights. He thought the lights were very poor and we took it to Moodie and Broderick's garage in Ennis. They soon discovered the problem and showed us how to put it on full beam. Joe also said, *'We are better to check this thing for oil while we are here.'* He lifted the bonnet at the front but quickly discovered there was no engine. The engine was at the back in the old Beetles. That was some of the teething problems we experienced. We had the car on hire for a couple of weeks and at the end of the hire period we were both pretty good drivers and felt that we didn't require any more driving lessons! At that time the roads in Ireland didn't have a lot of traffic. We returned to London and I hired a car there from time to time on my Irish driving licence and I have been driving ever since.

On another occasion we both returned home for Christmas and once again hired out a car sharing the costs. During the holiday period we had a heavy snowfall and a severe frost. Joe went to visit a former girlfriend who lived in a rather remote area. He asked me to accompany him. The lane leading to her house had snow and ice. The farmhouse was off the main road and downhill, so we didn't have a problem on the way in. When we were leaving it was a different story in that we couldn't get out of the lane. We left the car and started to walk and we walked for miles before we managed to get a lift, as cars were few and far between. The car was blocking the lane but we couldn't get back to retrieve it for a couple of days. When we returned to collect it the farmer and some of his neighbours assisted in getting us out. It was a rather bad experience. We travelled quite a lot to dances over the holiday period as petrol wasn't expensive.

For some returning home was more difficult than when they originally left and the frequency of visits became less and less when their parents passed away and when nobody was left in the old homestead. It was indeed so sad that the people that had to take the emigration route didn't have a home to return to. Many had this experience over the years.

For some a return visit to their old home could be more painful than when they left originally. Such was the experience of a man I heard of called Mick. He left home in the mid 1940s about the end of World War 11. It was nigh on thirty-five years since his last trip to his native County Clare. He was now on the wrong side of seventy so his wife Mary and family insisted that it was time for him to make the pilgrimage. The family took him to Burton's tailors to get him measured for a new suit. At that time the width of trouser leg bottoms were rather generous at twenty eight to thirty inches. Mick went for a brown coloured suit, with the wide trouser bottoms, waistcoat and a brown hat to match.

His last trip home was by boat from Holyhead to Dublin. This time the family paid the airfare for both of their parents, but Mick hadn't been on a plane before and felt a bit apprehensive. He had a few double Jamieson's and a couple of pints of the black stuff before they boarded the plane. Mary wanted to give him an extra bit of confidence and courage so she produced a bottle of Lourdes holy water. She gave him a good sprinkling before they boarded the plane saying, *'Now Mick this is a drop of Lourdes holy water and it will keep both of us safe.'* He said, *'I'll tell you something Mary I'd be a lot happier with a drop of Knock holy water.'*

On the plane he was seated near a window and a little while after take off he looked out and said, *'Oh God Mary we're very high off the ground. Do you know I've never been as high up as this before in my life.'* Mary said, *'Close your eyes Mick and say a little prayer to St. Christopher the Patron Saint of Travellers.'* He said, *'Well Mary, God only knows where St. Christopher is right now. Sure God 'tis years since I first heard about that fella and I never heard about him having anything to do with people travelling in aeroplanes and do you know what, sure God I don't think there were any aeroplanes around in his time. I've often heard the lads at work sayin' that he was alright up to sixty miles an hour for anybody driving a car but after that you're on your own. God Mary that man wouldn't know that we were goin' to Ireland.'* Mary said, *'Ah sure Mick we'll soon be there anyway.'* Mick pulled out a couple of miniature bottles of Jamieson's whiskey from the inside pocket of his jacket. He said, *'Mary I'll have a drop of Jamieson's holy water as I don't think the Lourdes water is strong enough to give me enough courage to finish the journey. I think the full strength Knock holy water would be better than that diluted Lourdes water. Sure when the girls were in Ireland they each brought back a big bottle of the Knock stuff, and it lasted a long time as it only took a small drop to do the job.'* On one occasion they made tea with it when the water was cut off and *'It tasted better than the water we get out of the taps in London.'*

When they arrived at Shannon airport they got a taxi to Limerick to catch a bus to Mick's home place. As they walked up the lane leading to the old house it was badly overgrown with briars and bushes. When the old skeleton of a cottage came into view, Mick's eyes welled up when he saw all that was left of it. Mary held his hand as he gazed in disbelief. The once brightly whitewashed cottage had become derelict with the thatched roof fallen in and doors and windows missing 'twas only a skeleton of the place he remembered from his young days. Briars were growing over the once whitewashed walls from the inside and the friendly welcoming family dog that once stood outside the front door wagging his tail had long since gone. For Mick it was like a shrine without the statues.

He could hardly speak and he stood there for a while in total shock as memories came flooding back of what was once the family home. With tears streaming down his face he turned to Mary saying, '*Do you know Mary 'tis hard lookin' at this 'tis worse for me than the first day I left home. Do you see where that bush is growing inside over there in the corner, well that was where I used to sleep.*' They couldn't get inside as briars and bushes had grown across the doorway. They then had a walk to the haggard and on the way there Mick was looking for the ducks' cabin but that was nowhere to be seen. He said, '*Mary do you know I can't think where the ducks' cabin was, but it was somewhere around here. I remember when I was a young lad I used to open the cabin door to let the ducks out. Sure god they'd head for the river for what we called the ducks' breakfast, a drink of water and a s...t.*' Of course the ducks' cabin had long since gone. He had a walk around the haggard now overgrown with bushes nettles and briars. He suddenly stopped and said, '*Mary will you take a look at the state of Paddy Pearce.*' It was an old Pearce mowing machine for cutting hay. It was submerged in nettles and briar badly rusted the wheels and seat missing. He said, '*God sure my father, rest his soul, cut many an acre of hay with that machine and his pair of horses.*' He then found the remains of an old spring tooth harrow and the axle of an old horse cart both submerged in nettles and long grass.

Then in the distance he heard the call of the Corncrake. He said, '*Ah sure 'tis nice to hear the corncrake, it must be 50 odd years since I last heard that lad.*' Mary said. '*Sure you wouldn't hear them in London with the noise of the traffic and I doubt if they have any corncrakes over there and anyway they'd sound different to Irish corncrakes.*' Mick had seen and heard enough and said, '*Mary I won't be back here again. This trip has brought back terrible memories when I look around and think back to how things were. We'll have a walk back to the front of the auld cottage and you can take a photo of me standing outside the front door.'* By the time they reached the front of the old cottage Mick was on his second handkerchief after he had also used a good lot of Mary's tissues. Mary took his photo and a few others of the surrounding area. Mick shed a few more tears, turned round and had another look at the remains of his old cottage.

A few new houses had sprung up in the neighbourhood since Mick's last visit. As they walked down the lane hand in hand Mick thought he'd make himself known by calling at one of the new houses as he wished to have a chat with somebody that might be able to fill in the missing years. He knocked on the door of the house nearest his old home. A young man and his wife greeted them. Mick explained the purpose of his visit to the neighbourhood and his past history and then introduced his wife Mary. They were both invited in for a cup of tea. The young couple explained that they moved into the area some years ago. The housewife introduced them to her dad Martin who was a bit older than Mick. Martin said, *'Sit down, sit down and we'll have an old chat.'* He then said, *'You'll drink an auld bottle of Stout.'* Mick thanked him and enjoyed the bottle of stout as they discussed old times. Martin asked him how they had travelled from London and Mick said that they had come by plane. He then added that they wouldn't be making the return journey by that devil of a plane as they were too high up for his liking and that he couldn't even have a walk outside to stretch his legs. Martin then said, *'No doubt you'll have seen big changes around here since you were last home.'* Mick explained the shock of seeing his old cottage home in such a derelict state and no family member to welcome him was a bit overwhelming. Mary had a cup of tea with the young housewife and explained to her how difficult the visit was for Mick. Martin said to Mick, *'You'll have another auld bottle of stout. Sure god only knows when we'll see you again.'* Mick declined the offer and thanked him for his hospitality and they went on their way.

Mick and Mary had a few days holiday in Kerry with Mary's sister Eileen. He said, *'We'll get the train to Dublin and have a couple of days there and then we'll get the auld boat back, as I didn't like that devil of a plane comin' over. We were too high up for my liking.'*

143

The visit home was a sad experience for Mick, possibly more painful than when he first left. This situation was typical of many emigrants that lost touch with home for decades and no parents or family member to return to. Mick was fortunate to have a wife and family as there were many who finished up alone.

When he got back to London he was telling the family about his experiences but he said, *'I'm glad I went but I won't be back there again. God when I think of my young days growin' up there and nothing left there now.'* His eyes welled up yet again and he thanked the family for making it possible for him to make the journey, and then he turned to Mary saying, *'Sure God I'd never have managed on my own, but the auld drop of Jamieson and the splash of holy water done the job.'* Mick's story illustrates the curse of emigration for countless thousands down through the decades and is still on-going. The sacrifices made by many emigrants have been forgotten about as the legacy of emigration continues to blight so many families.

Some men settled well in their new country worked hard and were very enterprising. It was back in the late 1950s early 1960s a gentleman called Timmy O' Riordan lived in Harrow Wealdstone, London. He had an allotment out in the Pinner area where he grew potatoes and vegetables. He had an old shed in the allotment and got the idea that he could keep chickens there.

Timmy was home in Sligo on holiday and he decided to take back some day old chicks to London with him. He was in his home town market where the day old chicks were sold. He bought a box that contained about a dozen chicks. The box had air holes. He took the chicks back to his parent's home as he still had a few days to go before returning to London. Finally Timmy set of for London by train and boat with his chicks. Everything went well 'till he got to London Euston, when the chicks were confiscated. Poor Timmy was rather disappointed but it didn't deter him from putting chickens in his allotment. He purchased a hen and a cockerel from a poultry farm and hatched some eggs. Eventually he hatched a lot of chicks in his allotment and added a couple of more sheds. He then started selling free range eggs and they were in big demand by the Irish community. He then sold chicken manure to people that had allotments in that area. He used to say, *'Ah sure a man has to try something to get himself a few bob.*' I suppose he could be described as enterprising Timmy!

It is true, however, that some Irishmen finished up in Doss or Routing houses. Camden Town and Elephant and Castle had such accommodation. These were places where men had a roof over their head, but precious little else. The people who finished up in one of these places were men that had no family or friends and were usually sleeping rough. The sad thing was that when they passed away they ended up in a pauper's grave without family or friends to mourn their passing. There are still some old men living lonely lives in hostels in some of the big cities but they are getting fewer as each year passes. They were men that worked hard, drank and gambled and gradually the years crept up on them. Their drinking buddies, the contractors that they sweated and worked hard with and for, and the pub landlords are all gone and so is their hard earned cash. Their legacy is living out their days in some old hostel. Many are suffering from rheumatism and arthritis from cold and wettings that they endured during their working days. A sad example of how many fine Irishmen finished up in a foreign land.

25. Life after London

My story of working in Britain continues right down through the decades. My friend Johnny and I started moving away from London from about mid 1957 although we had been out of London working on term contracts some short and some of reasonable duration with sub-contractors. We'd return to London at weekends whenever possible as the craic was always good and social life outside London just wasn't the same.

Our first big move was to Newark near Nottingham. It was excavating holes for pylons that would carry thirty-three thousand volt electric cables cross country. A lorry picked us up each morning in Nottingham and took us out to various sites. It was an old army truck and a four wheel drive for travelling across fields and rough terrain. Johnny a Donegal man was the driver and was very helpful and in the evening he conveyed men right to their accommodation. The old truck was a kind of night safe for our *'office'* equipment. All our digging tools - forks, shovels and picks, were stored in the back under an old tarpaulin at night along with our *'office'* attire such as wellington boots, donkey jackets, foot irons and our *'Irish safety helmets'*

It was hand excavation and some of the holes were up to 10 feet in depth. Stages were used where excavations were at a depth greater than six feet, as it became very difficult to throw the excavated material out. Where two stages were necessary the excavated material was passed from the bottom stage to the top one and it became very slow progress. It could be dangerous working at the bottom of the excavation when the excavated material began to pile up at the top. Martin Flannery or Flaherty, a Galway man, sustained a serious injury when a stone rolled off the top and hit him on the head. He had a pretty large gash which required a number of stitches but was fortunate that it wasn't more serious. His *'Irish safety helmet'* didn't offer much protection. He had a number of days off work which meant a loss of wages.

Some days we'd work without a break as we wouldn't have transport to take us to a shop or café to get something to eat. There weren't any facilities on-site or shelter when it rained and some evenings we'd arrive back at our accommodation and our clothes would be soaking wet, and nowhere to dry them. We had rented a room in a big property that had a number of other rooms, all rented to Irishmen who were mostly working on the same contract. In the room next to Johnny and I was a Donegal man and a Mayo man.

The Donegal man Owen Boyle, (his Monday to Friday name as he used to say) came from a remote area. His parents had passed away and his brother was at home in the farm. They were hill farmers with sheep only. He couldn't read or write and his brother had difficulty spelling and writing. One night he came into our room and he had a number of letters that he had received from his brother. They were addressed to an old address which he previously had in London. A friend of his who went to London at weekends had also lived at the old London address and had called to check if there was any mail for him. The landlady gave him a number of letters for Owen. It was rather sad that he couldn't read his brother's letters. He asked if we could read them to him. Johnny read a couple with difficulty and I tried to read some others. They didn't contain a lot of news but one letter had news about an uncle and one of his neighbours that had passed away. That made him really sad and he sat and cried. He asked us to write a few lines to his brother and explain about how bad he had been with the 'salvation flu', which was his name for the Asian flu. He asked not to put the address that he was living at, as he would have moved on by the time his brother replied. Owen said, '*God my uncle Tommy was such a good man. When my father died, rest his soul, Tommy took over and helped to bring us up.*' He then asked if one of us could get a Mass card and send it to Tommy's wife. He gave Johnny a couple of pounds to get a card and have it signed by a priest and he also gave him an address to send it to. He was very grateful for our help.

The work was cross country adjacent to fields growing farmer's crops such as grain and spuds. Some of the bigger farmers were helpful in that they made available some of their farm produce free of charge. We always took some potatoes, cabbage, onions and turnip back to the accommodation so it was only a case of purchasing a big piece of bacon to grease the cabbage, as they would say.

The smell of bacon and cabbage cooking made one a bit homesick. The cooking was a bit rough and it wouldn't be to the standards of The Ritz Hotel. Two gas cookers were available, one on the ground floor and one on the first floor. The cookers or cooking utensils weren't cleaned very often. The men were big and rough and mostly from the West of Ireland. A couple could easily sink a stone of spuds between them in a sitting and sometimes they would bring in a few bottles of Guinness from the pub. The spuds were usually big and floury with the jackets bursting. After they had their meal it might end up with a bit of a sing song although there would still be a good pile of potato peelings on the table, but washing up dishes wasn't a priority. At the weekends most lads tried to tidy things up, but there were a couple who never made any effort. Rooms could be very untidy as some men left things on the floor, such as dirty washing and their old suitcase with items of clothing hanging out of them. Bed covers were dirty as some men lay on top of them with their old working clothes. It was the year of the Asian flu 1957, and just about everybody living in that house had the flu at the same time. My friend Johnny and I couldn't get out of bed to make a cup of tea. It took us all our time to get to the toilet. For a couple of days, all we had to drink was water and it was much the same for the others. It wasn't too surprising that we got the Asian flu when one considers the conditions that we were working and living in. The house was like a hospital but without doctors or nurses. A total of nine men all in bed with a very bad flu and nobody had a doctor to call on. The landlord asked his doctor to come in and check everybody out, but it emerged that the contractor was not paying the block NHS insurance that he alleged he was paying on behalf of his employees. Each of us had to pay the landlord's doctor to attend to us. From memory I think it was only £3 each. The contractor was prosecuted for deception and also for tax evasion. It was at times such as this that one really missed family; lying in bed and nobody to get medication or even a cup of tea. When we were well enough we all returned to London.

My next outing from London was to Edenbridge town in Kent. My cousin Tony and Mick and John Enright from Kerry worked with me. Cousin Tony was a great man who did well in life. He set up his own company which was very successful. He treated and paid his men very well and had many friends. The Enright brothers were good workers and nice people. John usually got dressed up at night after he had something to eat and would go out for a couple of pints. He had a brown suit and one night when he was getting dressed he looked at the suit and said, '*I think my bit of brown is getting a bit foolish looking.*' meaning that he had worn it that often. The work was based on production and paid by results. I think it was for the installation of a water main. Cousin Tony and I lived in digs with full board and lodging. After we'd have our evening meal, we sometimes went back to the job to do a bit more work and might work to about eight o'clock backfilling the excavation where the main-laying was complete. It was heavy going for the rate of pay we were getting.

Our next job was a large excavation in High Wycombe. Again it was a paid by results job. The excavation was a pumping station for a sewer and the dimensions were 42 .6″ x 26 .6 .6″ x 20 in depth. We were paid £1 per cubic yard for excavating chalk and flint. The water table was very high and necessitated the continuous use of 2 x 6 inch water pumps. Friday was measure up day and we were always short measured, so inevitably it resulted in arguments.

It was towards the end of the 1950s, in the months of October and November a number of men, me included, were recruited to carry out excavation work for the installation of a thirty-three thousand volt cable on the outskirts of Tewksbury, Gloucestershire and ended up being rescued by boat! We had been working on another big contract in South Wales that employed over forty men. All the men who were on that contract returned to London when it finished. We had accommodation in Cheltenham, not too far from Tewksbury, and we were working some distance from the nearest road.

An old ex-army four wheel drive truck took us across some rough ground each day to the site where we were working. Most country lanes and roads at that time weren't surfaced and they were kind of dirt tracks. At that time, it was all hand excavation and I believe there were eleven men in the squad. Some of the well-known characters that followed cable laying jobs were Goose

Pimple O'Reilly from Cavan, The Horse Connolly from Galway, Blondie O'Shea from Kerry and a few others. Of course the names listed wouldn't be correct as most men in that type of utility work were working incognito at that time, and so was I. We were working adjacent to the mighty River Severn near to where the River Avon adjoins.

It had rained for almost a week, day and night, with the odd exception and the river became badly swollen. Some other big rivers that flow into the Severn were also swollen. It flooded a large area of the countryside in and around the Tewksbury area and we became marooned in a field. The water levels rose rapidly and closed in from all directions. The driver of the truck tried to get us out but there was no escape route as the water was too deep. He managed to reverse back to dry ground but we had to abandon the truck and walk to a farmhouse some distance away. It was raining and getting dark. Needless to say we were soaking wet and cold and hungry. We explained our predicament to the farmer, so he gave us permission to use some old outhouses and a hay barn. Both him and his wife were very nice people and did what they could for us. He didn't have a telephone or any means of communication with the outside world.

The farmer and his wife made tea and gave us some food, but because of numbers it only amounted to a small portion for each man. Some men were very hungry as nobody had very much to eat during the day. For those who smoked and usually had a drink after work, the situation was rather grim. The water was closing in on the farmyard from all directions. Apparently all that area had been flooded on a number of occasions over the years. It was two days before we were rescued. The electricity went off the second night and the whole area was in darkness. However, the farmer was using candles in the farm house. One of the occupants in the hayshed managed to make his way across to the farm house to ask for a candle. The farmer refused as he felt it was too dangerous to have a naked light in a shed almost full of hay. He gave him an old torch, but the batteries were low and didn't last very long. It was scary in the darkness as one couldn't keep check on the rising water levels.

Sleeping in the hay barn on straw beds in the lofts of the old outhouses wasn't exactly comfortable, but better than being stranded in flood water out in the fields. At night it got very cold, because the men's clothes and the wellington boots were wet and cold. The first night that we took refuge, water flooded the farmyard and surrounding area and it entered some of the outhouses. Water also entered the farm house. Luckily, we were all wearing wellington boots and we were able to walk across the farmyard to the farm house to collect hot drinks. The hot drinks were tea and cocoa and helped a little bit, but hunger was the main problem. Next morning we didn't have anything to eat by way of a proper breakfast, but we got tea from the farmer and his wife gave us some home-made cakes. Of course they too had become very low in food rations after their generosity the previous evening. The farmer had some turnip in one of the outhouses and some desperate men ate them raw, and a few suffered the consequences. Blondie O'Shea commented, '*Sure Jaysus we never thought when we left home we'd end up eating raw turnip.*' A couple of characters amongst the squad kept spirits up a little by singing songs and telling jokes. The farmer had an orchard and there were still some cooking apples on a couple of the trees. Some of the men ate cooking apples and turnip as part of their diet - the only things available.

A few of the men got rather anxious as they hadn't any idea how they were going to get out of the situation they were in. A couple of men suffered from diarrhoea due to being wet and cold and resulting from a rather unusual food diet. Toilet facilities were also a problem as the area around the outdoor toilet was flooded. It had to be back to the open air facilities again wherever one could find a little patch that wasn't under water with freshly grown toilet paper.

The local Tewksbury fire service was unable to assist as the town was cut off. Over a two day period neighbouring fire services from Cambridge and Gloucester areas, and perhaps further afield visited all properties that were cut off and they used boats to reach farm houses. The boat which came to our rescue was only a small rowing boat and could only carry a few men on each rescue attempt. The rescue of people from all the cut off properties including Tewksbury town was an immense task and was time consuming and all the more difficult without the aid of helicopters.

They started our rescue operation by taking just a few men each time to the nearest road which was almost a mile away. It took all day to get everybody out. After the first trip, they brought some food back for the remaining men. For people who were cut off, food was arranged and made available by the Salvation Army. The farmer, his wife, dogs and cats were also rescued from the marooned property where we took refuge. He lost some of his livestock such as sheep, cattle and a couple of pigs.

It was a week before the water had drained sufficiently to recover the ex-army truck. All work associated with the cable laying project was abandoned due to the flooding. The contractor laid on transport to take us to Gloucester and arranged accommodation free of charge for one night. The landlord of an Irish pub in Gloucester gave us food and organised dry clothing from nearby charity shops. The day after, the rescue one of the main news items in a local newspaper was about the Irishmen that were rescued by boat from flooding in the Tewksbury area. We all returned to London the evening after the rescue. It was another item to add to the catalogue of experiences of working in the construction and utilities industries.

Perhaps one might ask why Irishmen travelled out of London and other big cities and towns to work throughout England, Wales and Scotland. First and foremost Irishmen were kind of nomads, the wandering type, as opposed to their British counterparts. British men would have local ties, such as the girlfriend or a local football team to support. Also they were more refined than Paddy and not used to the rough and tumble life that their Irish counterparts were accustomed to. Heavy, dirty labouring work was not for them. Some English local labour would be employed as drivers or members of office staff albeit for short periods.

Of course for most young Irishmen who had left Ireland to work in Britain it didn't matter too much where they worked and lived for a number of years while they remained single. They were always willing to move at short notice. Sometimes moving long distances caused problems such as having to pay rent up front, laundry that hadn't been collected or not ready for collection, and mail from home. For people leaving London, Birmingham or Manchester and moving to Scotland or Wales it wouldn't be cost effective to return to collect mail or laundry. It could be up to six months before it would be possible to make the return journey as they may be working seven days per week.

The many areas and sites that I worked in throughout Britain such as Kent, Nottingham, South Wales and Scotland were mostly with Irishmen, particularly the utilities industries. Local labour weren't interested in that type of work and wouldn't be prepared to work in the austere site conditions that Paddy worked in. It was mostly Irish sub-contractors that were engaged in that type of work. In some cases, the bigger sub-contractors would come to an arrangement with an English company about tendering for particular contracts. It would be rather difficult for sub-contractors to tender directly to some of the big utility companies as they wouldn't be in a position to fulfil some of the specifications such as insurance, expertise and capital outlay. When a contract was awarded to the successful company, the sub-contractor then supplied labour and plant to carry out the excavation and reinstatement work. He'd generally employ Irishmen, as they wouldn't be members of a trade union, would be prepared to work hard and were easy to exploit. The parent company would carry out the technical work such as cable jointing, testing and commissioning. Because many sub-contractors evaded tax and insurance for their employees, it was possible to put in lower tender bids to secure the work. Hence the reason British sub-contractors found it difficult to be competitive with tenders. Local labour wouldn't be interested working incognito to avoid paying tax and insurance or losing out on benefits such as sick pay and holiday pay.

I also worked in Sandwich in Kent with two Tipperary brothers, Patsy and Billy Quinlan. They were very nice people and Patsy always had a smile. We'd return to London for the weekend to socialise with our friends. My friend Johnny and I worked for De Lacy around the Chesterfield area and got accommodation in Fairfield Road, Chesterfield. It was pretty basic but we seldom had meals there.

It was mostly Monday to Friday, as we usually returned to London at weekends for the craic. Train fares were inexpensive at that time. It was a cable contract but only for a short duration of about a couple of months. We seemed to be always living out of a suitcase in that we were moving from place to place. Having worked around Birmingham and Manchester and other cities and towns throughout the UK, life for Irish communities was pretty synonymous with the Irish in London; but I think it would be fair to say that London was the main Irish hub in Britain.

26.
Scotland and Wales

In June 1959 De Lacy, or it may have been Bartholomew, were recruiting men for a big gas pipeline contract in Scotland. Regardless which one it was they were both familiar names as London sub-contractors. They were offering attractive rates of pay as it was pretty difficult to get men to leave London to work in Scotland. It was a long term contract with a paid weekend off every six weeks and fares and travelling expenses were paid.

Johnny my friend and a number of others volunteered to go. We left London by train for Edinburgh, a journey of about four hundred miles. We then got a train over the Forth Bridge to Dunfermline. We were picked up there and taken to Falkirk to look for accommodation. It was another new world trying to understand the local lingo but the people were friendly and welcoming. The job was a forty five miles gas pipeline from Westfield in Fife to Coatbridge in Lanarkshire. Some of the others in the team were, the Graven brothers three fine men from Achill Island, County Mayo, Mick, Jimmy and Tom all RIP They were all very good machine men and good friends of mine. Between them they operated a big machine called a Cleveland excavator and they manned it night and day. It was a big American monster that could eat up ground. It was capable of excavating one mile of trench a day up to a depth of eight feet. A special feature was that as the material was excavated it went on to a conveyor belt and deposited six feet away from the edge of the excavation. It served two purposes in that it kept the weight of the excavated material away from the edge of the excavation and made provision for the sections, lengths of pipeline, to be placed adjacent to the excavation for welding. The Graven brothers were also very good operators of other heavy machinery.

I remember Mick had a left hand drive car and I think it was an American model. I recall the registration number being OBO 507. They'd drive the car across fields, sometimes getting stuck. They were big strong men and they'd soon lift or push the car out of where it stuck and get it on its way again. Like me, Mick married a Falkirk Lass who was a friend of my wife..

The other people that I remember who travelled north to Scotland were, Tom Gilboy, Martin Philbin and John Fleming, all from County Mayo. John Padian and another man whose name I forget, from County Roscommon. The famous Cockney Daly, Joe Daly was from County Donegal. Coleman O'Donnell and Martin Walsh were from County Galway. There were others whose names I don't remember. Most of the men named above lived around the town of Falkirk. It was a bit difficult to get accommodation. However, Johnny, me and a Roscommon chap got accommodation from a Mrs McGhee, 4 Argyll Avenue.

Others settled for hostels that locally were called Models. They were pretty basic types of accommodation, but some men preferred living in them as opposed to digs. They were a cheap form of accommodation and mostly used by men endeavouring to save money to send home. In some cases they had cubicles partitioned off as their sleeping quarters, but they weren't sound proof. They were mostly used by men working in the construction and utilities industries. Some men returned to their accommodation with just the clothes that they had been working in all day, including wellington boots. McGregors was situated near the Public Baths and the Livingstonia in Kerse Lane. There was also the Thornhill Hostel in Thornhill Road near the Victoria Park. They had little shops incorporated where it was possible to purchase bits and pieces. Hot plates were the order of the day for cooking on. A number of men could cook at the same time. It was possible to smell the cooking as one passed by. The area for cooking was a kind of meeting place where men discussed their day's activities. Although it was mostly Donegal men that lived in the Falkirk Models, there were some men from Kerry, Galway and Mayo and a couple from Clare. They weren't ideal living conditions as food, clothing and money were stolen from time to time, but they were places of freedom in that one could come and go as one pleased.

For anybody living in the Falkirk area and liked a drink on a Sunday, it was necessary to go to another area at least two miles away. At that time, pubs were closed on a Sunday and only hotels were licensed to sell alcohol, but one would have to be a bona fide traveller. Of course like everything else there was a way round things. The Irishmen working on the above contract and living in Falkirk got drink in some Hotels in Falkirk. They were new to the town and the fact that they mostly lived in hostels meant they weren't known in the town. They'd say they had travelled from somewhere else outside the town and were only passing through and that made them bona fide travellers. Going to Ireland on holiday from Scotland involved a long sea journey from Glasgow to Dublin. I once sailed from Anderson Quay, Glasgow to North Wall Pier, Dublin. It was a thirteen to fourteen hour journey and it was a very rough crossing. I believe it was the only sea crossing between Scotland and the Republic of Ireland at that time. As the boat sailed down the Clyde it stopped at Whiteinch to load cattle. All night long the cattle were bellowing as they were tossed about in rough seas. They were in the hold down below and it was possible to smell them up on deck. I think that some cattle were injured during that crossing and had to be destroyed. Many people had to sit on their cases all night as there wasn't enough seating. It was very slow in comparison to the high-speed ships that currently operate between Britain and Ireland.

Facilities on board were a bit primitive in that hot meals were not available, at least on that crossing. People were sick all night and spent most of the night in the toilets. Doors kept banging as the boat was tossed about from one side to the other in mountainous seas. There was no heating and the lights went out so people had to sit in cold and darkness for a number of hours until the lights were restored. No hot drinks were available. When we got to Dublin, the boat couldn't dock at North Wall due to high winds. Some people were very ill and had to be taken off. I don't know how they were taken off. It was a terrible experience for women with young children.

The return journey was equally as bad and, once again, there were cattle on board. As the boat moved up the Clyde it stopped at Whiteinch again to offload the cattle. Then it proceeded up the Clyde to Anderson Quay. I had a few more journeys from Glasgow to Dublin on that slow boat. The journey from Glasgow to Limerick took approximately eighteen to twenty hours. Nowadays, Glasgow to Shannon takes about an hour or an hour and a half maximum by air, but again I don't think that there were direct flights from

Glasgow to Shannon at that time. I think the Glasgow to Dublin boat service was discontinued around the end of the 1960s.

At the end of 1960 or early 1961, after the Scotland contract finished, I moved to South Wales to work on another gas contract. It was a thirty-six inches gas pipeline into Llanwern Steel Works. I got accommodation at 5 Bolt Street, Newport. A lot of Irish were working on big sites around the Cardiff and Swansea areas. It was difficult to get rented accommodation in these areas at that time. For those that were in rented accommodation it was much the same procedure as London. After work most men would go straight to the pub. However, some would be too topped up and fell asleep in the pub and wouldn't be going anywhere except upstairs. Some landlord's would have a couple of rooms upstairs with kind of bed settees for such occasions. Getting the one or two that had fallen asleep up to the rooms would be a problem as they were big heavy men. Men staying in the pub overnight would be to the landlord's advantage. Next morning they wouldn't go to work, so they'd buy breakfast in the pub and then start an early drinking shift after they had carried out a full audit of their finances. Sometimes they'd get a sub from the landlord, which meant that they'd have to get a sub at night from one of their mates to pay back the landlord. Some wouldn't lose a day's wages by not going to work, as the site foreman would book them in as having worked the day. He would be a '*good*' friend of theirs and in return he'd get a cut of the day's wages and a couple of drinks in the pub. Most big sites had a lot of men so a few taking days off work over a long period meant everybody was in pocket. Booking in so called '*dead men*' or '*ghost men*' was also another nice little earner.

I shared a room with a Connemara man, but sometimes he'd say he was from Kerry, who topped up with pints of bitter most nights. He could drink up to ten pints and because his plumbing wasn't too good it meant a lot of visits to the toilet throughout the night. It was an outside toilet down the backyard. There wasn't an outside light and one night he went into the garden shed that was adjacent to the toilet. He deposited whatever it was in the shed and, of course, the following evening when he returned from work the landlady confronted him. She had put his bag outside the door ready to evict him. He was adamant that he used the toilet, but it ended up a shouting match. He finally persuaded her to give him another chance and they did a bit of a compromise

To avoid outdoor journeys through the night the landlady kindly put a receptacle under his bed. He'd use matches to avoid putting on the light as he felt that he might disturb me and so he was busy most nights lighting matches at regular intervals. Overnight he kept the receptacle on top of a small locker at the side of his bed so it was a permanent stand for it even during use. With a lighted match in one hand, and shall we say something else in the other hand, it was rather astonishing that there wasn't a burning incident. The downside was the receptacle wasn't large enough for the volume resulting in accidents. The landlady gave him a second vessel to avoid overflows and spillage. She was French and didn't have a lot of English and the gentleman in question preferred to speak in Gaelic so the conversations between them were a bit strained to say the least, particularly anytime there was an accident. It was his job each morning to empty the containers in the outside toilet and that meant going through the landlady's kitchen. One morning, as he was going through her kitchen, there was a bit of spillage. They were shouting at each other and neither knew what the other was saying. They finally parted company after the gentleman had an accident in bed. That was about 1961.

I went back to work in Scotland during the 1960s and '70s. Again some companies and sub-contractors used similar methods in tax avoidance to their English counterparts. This applied to most of the utility companies. Some contractors' supervisors who secured long-term contracts with utility companies worked in partnership with the utilities supervisors and senior personnel, using the *'brown envelope'* system. A lot of jobs were done on a day-work basis and again *'dead men'* were signed for by the utilities supervisors in return for a share of the money. Mostly all of the contractor's employees were paid by the shift. Some companies or contractors supplying men on a day-work basis, charged some utility companies for imported labour. They were able to secure a better hourly day-work rate as they had allegedly imported the labour directly from Ireland specifically for a given contract due to the unavailability of skilled local labour. The contractors were paying lodging allowance to the men they had imported from Ireland. Of course the so called imported labour was Irishmen who had lived in Scotland for a number of years. They weren't paid lodging allowance except on the odd occasion when it was necessary to travel to some remote areas in the north and west of Scotland. It was brown envelopes for the supervisors and brown envelopes for the contractor's agents. The contractor benefited from the revenue accrued from lodging allowance claimed but not paid. The utility's supervisors and the contractor's agents shared the spoils of the revenue associated with booking of so called '*dead men*' and '*ghost items of plant*'.

In the late 1960s and early 1970s I was involved in the conversion programme of town gas to natural gas. A couple of English companies secured most of the conversion work in Scotland although there were a number of other contractors. I was a foreman qualified to work on live gas operations. The qualification was GD4 and 5 mains and services. The GD4 qualification was a requirement by Scottish Gas and British Gas before one was allowed to install pipelines, pressure test, commission pipelines or work on live gas operations. The GD5 qualification was necessary for the installation of domestic or commercial services, also to pressure test, make connections to live mains and commission the services. Most operatives had dual qualifications.

Before work could proceed on the commissioning of the mains network with natural gas preliminary work had to be carried out. This was the installation of isolation valves and sector proving. A lot of this work was carried out at night-time and weekends when customer demand for gas was low. It was then possible to reduce pressures on medium and high pressure mains. There was plenty overtime work and also a time when a lot of money changed hands between some sub- contractors and some utility personnel. To insert a valve in a live main it was necessary to flow stop the gas. This involved a bypass to carry the gas across the isolated section and keep the main live either side. Sometimes mains were dual flow or two way fed. A flow stop at that time was what was termed '*open bagging*'. Holes had to be drilled in the live main to insert the bags, and I think, from memory, the bags were made of canvas. To insert a bag into a live main the plug had to be removed and the neatly folded bag inserted through the plug hole. The bag was then inflated by a bag pump to stop the gas flow but bags didn't have pressure gauges fitted. The dangerous part of the operation was when a section of pipe was removed from the isolated section leaving open ends. If a bag or bags suddenly burst or deflated it caused a cessation or pressure loss within the live main to the point where air mixed with the gas and became an explosive mixture.

When that took place it caused major problems as the main couldn't be re-commissioned until all customers supplied from that section were contacted, their supply pipe purged and their appliances checked. It was necessary to double bag either side of the section to be isolated. Some old mains had heavy deposits of corrosion on the inside making it difficult to get a tight flow stop. The bypass had a valve at either end. Additional holes would be drilled in the main, either side of the flow stops, to facilitate water gauges and recorders to monitor the pressure. To check if a main was dual flow, two-way fed, it was necessary to slowly close a bypass valve and monitor the pressure either side. If it was only a one way feed the pressure would quickly drop on the side dependant on the bypass.

Of course everybody in the excavation, involved in the operation wore a gas mask. Flow stopping could be a very dangerous operation and while working on live gas there were many accidents particularly while working with the old town gas. People were gassed or badly burnt in the event of a fire.

The drilling of live mains and flow stop operations became gas free with the introduction of the WASK (supplier of pipes and fitments) equipment. The drilling machine was called a *'Tee Set'* and the flow stop equipment *'Bag Pipes'*. Of course it wasn't possible to play them like the Scottish or Irish versions! Flow stopping a medium pressure main involved reducing the pressure to about 2PSI (two pounds per square inch). Again, the flow stop operation wasn't gas free and it involved inserting Peden (name of supplier) Stoppers through three or four inch holes that had been drilled in the main with gas blowing at 2PSI.

It was an extremely dangerous operation particularly if the escaping gas was accidentally ignited. That operation became gas free with the introduction of Stopple Off Equipment which was

161

usually carried out by the Gas Board's own employees. Stopple Off Equipment was used to stop the flow of gas through a pipeline to enable carrying out a particular operation such as cutting out a section of pipe and renewing or to terminating a pipeline and fitting a cap end. First of all a tee piece had to be fitted to the pipe. It was two halves bolted together with rubber seals and when fitted it totally encapsulated the area of pipe that it covered. One of the halves would have a flanged junction to facilitate a valve. When the valve was fitted both valve and tee were pressure tested with air. Sometimes, the pressure test could be up to one hundred pounds per square inch. The next step of the operation would be to cut a hole into the pipe through the valve. It would be necessary to cut away the top part of the pipe to insert the stopple equipment inside. The stopple was like a disc and, when inserted and turned inside the pipe, sealed off the flow of gas but that was only part of the operation. In some cases it would be necessary to fit a bypass to carry the gas over the isolated section, and recorders to monitor pressures. The small diameter cast iron mains, three and four inch, were replaced with polyethylene pipe following the King Report (1977), particularly where these mains were laid in close proximity to properties. It followed a series of explosions up and down the country involving a number of fatalities. The old cast iron mains were susceptible to radial fractures particularly in very frosty conditions or where they were laid too close to the surface. The mains replacement programme created a lot of employment for a number of years.

27.
I Settle For Scotland!

Back in the 1950s, '60s and '70s Irishmen and women endured a lot of hardship endeavouring to make a living in distant lands and trying to assist struggling family members left behind in Ireland. Many settled in Britain and America and remained there.

I met my wife, Bridgetta at a St. Patrick's night dance on March 17th 1960. At that time there were quite a few Irish living in and around the Falkirk area. I wasn't very familiar with the Scottish accent at that time. After I danced with my wife-to-be, I invited her for a mineral. Of course she wasn't familiar with the word *'mineral'* as they referred to it as a *'soft drink'*. When I asked her she replied *'I donna ken.'* which I found out meant *'I don't know.'* We married on May 5th 1962. Our family are a bit scattered. We have a daughter in America, a daughter in Northern Ireland, a son in Southern Ireland and three daughters in Scotland. Our daughter Frances, husband and family are about to emigrate to Australia.

A couple of other Irish emigrants also met their wives in Falkirk. Michael Graven that I mentioned earlier married a Falkirk Lass as did a couple of others. Three of my wife's sisters married three Clare men, allegedly as a result of my marriage to Bridgetta; so four Falkirk sisters married four Clare men. They used to holiday in Lissycasey so Patricia RIP met and married John Hanrahan RIP a Lissycasey man. The Hanrahan's are well recognised for music and dance. Eileen married a Gerry Connellan from Ennis. Gerry was into house building for a number of years. A school friend of mine Jerome Griffin RIP and a friend of his came to Scotland from London to visit me. He fell in love with Maria and Maria with him and they married in 1969. Jerome was a gentleman and a very dear friend. They moved to Ireland in the late 1970s and finished up in Ballyea where they bought some land. Another sister Kathleen married Thomas Cassidy a County Westmeath man. So there must be something about the Irish. My story about four Falkirk sisters marrying four Clare men featured in the local paper the *'Falkirk Herald'* in February 2013. It was headed *'Something about the Irish'*. It generated a lot of interest from people of Irish descent.

I hope you enjoy reading this book and that it will bring back many memories to those of you who shared the journey with me.

I have tried to give as broad and truthful a picture as possible of my journey as an emigrant and how the Irish worked and lived in Britain during the 1950s, '60s, '70s.

I was always glad that I made the journey.

Epilogue

Having lived and worked over the past 60 years in the United Kingdom I felt I had a story to tell about my experiences down through the decades. Perhaps it will help today's generation to understand the hardships and compromises that their parents and grand-parents who emigrated in the 1940s,'50s, and '60s had to endure down through the years. Also I thought my family would like to have it documented.

It has been a difficult journey at times but determination and hard work saw me through and I don't have any regrets. Yes, it was difficult leaving home but I now recognise that going to the UK at that time gave me opportunities that weren't available in Ireland during the era that I left.

My wedding in 1962 to Bridgetta Collins a native of Falkirk Scotland resulted in further emigration in that three of her sister's moved to County Clare and settled there. Bridgetta and I had seven children but James is deceased. We worked hard to rear and educate them. Bridgetta worked in the Health Service and she was a very good wife. Some of the family got the emigration bug perhaps it was hereditary. Teresa Mary moved to California, USA, Frances moved to Australia, Claire moved to Northern Ireland and Tony to the Republic. Ann Marie and Pauline still live in Scotland.

For a number of years after I arrived in Britain I was labouring in house building and then moved to the utilities industry working on cable, gas and water contracts. I worked in the construction and utilities industries throughout the UK. I made my home in Scotland, but worked south of the border for a number of years travelling back home at weekends.

After I married I felt the spade I was accustomed to using was getting heavy so I decided to get something lighter. I pushed on by going on courses and a bit of private tuition to get the necessary qualifications to work on live gas operations and associated work. Not content to continue doing that to the end of my working life, I progressed to become supervisor, manager and contracts manager. I was employed by a good Yorkshire company and I became Quality Manager. I then moved on to become Procurement

Manager and finished my working days as Audit Manager.

Bridgetta and I celebrated our Golden Wedding on May 5th 2012. I am still 100% Irish and always will be. My thoughts of the Benedin Hills to the rear of my old homestead and the River Shannon to the front, are pictures of my young days firmly fixed in my mind never to be erased.

Go raibh mile maith agat,
Joe Quinlivan

Acknowledgements

I would first and foremost like to thank my immediate and extended family for their love and support. Without them this project would not even have started.

My sincere thanks and gratitude go to Stella O'Gorman, Michael O'Gorman, Maureen Mescall and Nancy Creech for editing and restructuring the script. They were instrumental in getting this book published. Their patience, perseverance and attention to detail are incomprehensible.

I give a special thanks to Professor Cathal O'Donoghue for taking the time to write the preface for the book.

I am grateful to Colin Waugh of The Clancy Group for his kind donation to the cost of this book.

Other individuals I should like to thank for their advice, help and guidance are as follows : Tim Kelly, Ennis County Clare; Tom Kelleher, Fleetwood, Lancashire; Elizabeth Odell, Kodiak, Alaska; the McDonald sisters, Buffalo, New York; Patricia Reidy Lawrence and Elaine Kavanaugh, Croce, New York; Maureen Higgins, the Safe-Home Programme, County Mayo; John Corbett, (The Golden Pin), Gurteen, Ballinasloe, County Galway.

I should also like to thank the following people and their companies for making old pictures available and for allowing me to use them: Bridget French, Mark Sewell and Colin Waugh, The Clancy Group, Harefield, Middlesex, UK; Natalie Bosher, McNicholas, Elstree, Herts. UK; Yvonne Fertnig, Steve Landes, MJ Gleeson Group Dublin, Ireland; Justin Fitzgerald, the Murphy Group, Highgate London UK; Maureen Comber, Clare County Library, Ennis Co. Clare; Seamus Hayes, Clare Champion , Ennis. Michael Corcoran, President, Transport Museum Society of Ireland; Peter Higginbotham, author of the History of the Workhouse; Stephan Dickers, Library and Archives manager, Bishopsgate Institute; Bob

Collins, photographer; The Reynolds Family Collection of Irish Showbands. All these groups retain the copyright of the pictures displayed in this book.

Thank you to House of Names for allowing us to use their Quinlivan crest on the cover of this book

I would like to apologise in advance if I've omitted anybody from the list of acknowledgements that I should have included or inadvertently breached copyright of any pictures.